BUILDING BULLETIN 79

Passive solar schools

A Design Guide

Department for Education
Architects and Building Division

LONDON: HMSO

Acknowledgements
This bulletin is based on a research project carried out by the Applied Energy Department at Cranfield University. DFE would like to thank the following members of the research team:

    Colin Grindley
    Richard Barton
    Barbara Swann

The bulletin also draws on the earlier research carried out at Cranfield by Brian Norton (now at the University of Ulster at Jordanstown), Richard Hobday and Doug Harris. DFE would like to thank them for their work.

DFE would also like to thank members of the project Steering Group and Local Education Authorities who provided information on various schools. Thanks are also due to the Society of Chief Electrical and Mechanical Engineers (SCEME) and the Society of Chief Architects of Local Authorities (SCALA) for their help with the project.

DFE Project Team
Head of Section - M Patel
Senior Engineer - R Daniels
Senior Architect - R Bishop

Contents

Symbols used in this bulletin

Solar radiation including both the components of short wave and long wave radiation

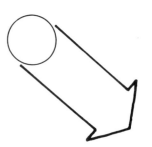

Natural ventilation

Mechanical ventilation

Long wave radiation

Convection

Thermal conduction

Summary

Solar energy is a renewable resource which can make a useful contribution to the heating and lighting of schools and has an important part to play in the UK Strategy for Sustainable Development. Even in our northern latitudes, we get a lot of sunshine, which if properly controlled, can help to reduce a school's energy bills.

Solar energy is also a non polluting source of energy. Thus its effective utilisation helps to reduce emissions of carbon dioxide and other gases resulting from the use of fossil fuels.

This bulletin describes the principles and practice of passive solar design as applied to design of new schools and also refurbishment of existing schools. It is largely aimed at the architects and engineers involved. It will also be of interest to building managers because it gives some idea of the various remodelling options.

The bulletin is based on a study carried out by Cranfield University for the DFE. The two main findings of the study are:

- Schools with passive solar features need not cost more than ordinary schools.

- A good passive solar school design can result in at least a 10% reduction in energy use.

Based on an analysis of monitored passive solar schools and computer simulation exercises carried out by the research team, the bulletin makes the following design recommendations:

- For significant winter solar gains the glazed apertures should face within 30^0 of due south.

- The axial orientation of a building, with a central atrium, has little effect on its energy usage.

- The width of a single storey atrium should not exceed 7 metres. This is to prevent excessive heat loss in winter and overheating in summer.

- To prevent summertime overheating, which can be a major problem in atria and conservatories, around 20% of the roof area should be openable.

- Overhangs of more than 300 mm over windows serve little purpose in terms of shading or improved daylighting.

It should be pointed out that this bulletin does not cover the wider issues of school design, in which respect meeting the educational needs should always have top priority. It should also be remembered that passive solar design is inherently climate specific and this bulletin deals only with locations with a British or Northern European climate.

Introduction

The sun's heat is an abundant and inexhaustible source of energy. Even in our northern latitudes, we get plenty of sunshine which can be used to reduce significantly our consumption of fossil fuels.

The UK Strategy for Sustainable Development published by the Government in January 1994, identified solar energy as an important non-polluting and renewable energy source. By making effective use of this we can limit environmental damage, conserve our fossil fuel reserves and save money.

School buildings offer many opportunities to use solar energy in a 'passive' way. A passive solar school absorbs and distributes solar energy by means of the form and fabric of the building. Solar energy usage can be improved by incorporating 'passive solar features' like atria and conservatories.

Effective utilisation of solar energy depends on factors like orientation, building materials, window design, shading, heating and lighting controls. It also depends on the usage of the spaces within the building. Hence, a good passive solar school design, one which both saves energy and creates pleasant environmental conditions in the school, is very difficult to achieve. There are many examples of schools where an atrium or other such feature has been incorporated into the design because of their popularity, without much thought of the consequences. Such schools often suffer from severe overheating in summer, and excessive heat loss and high fuel consumption in winter.

This bulletin offers advice on how to approach passive solar design and also offers some design recommendations.

The bulletin is based on a research project carried out by the Department of Applied Energy of Cranfield University for the DFE. The project involved investigating the energy behaviour of many existing passive solar schools in the UK, monitoring some of them and extensive computer modelling to test out various design options.

The bulletin covers both new and existing schools. While the opportunities for the passive solar design of new schools are obvious, it is important to remember that there are also opportunities for older schools. Amalgamation, refurbishment and remodelling are all opportunities to investigate the use of passive solar features in existing schools.

Chapter 2 of the bulletin describes the basic principles of passive solar design for schools.

Chapter 3 introduces some of the main passive solar features and looks at how these can be incorporated into designs and again offers guidance.

Chapter 4 provides an economic and energy appraisal, based on information collected during the research.

Chapter 5 includes case studies of some of the schools looked at by the research team. About 40 schools in all were investigated, of which 17 are included. The schools looked at fall within 3 categories.

Type A: Schools that are primarily of passive solar design.

Type B: Schools which include some passive solar feature.

Type C: Schools of some interest in the passive solar context.

The case studies in chapter 5 are all type A except for John Cabot CTC and Leith Academy which are type B.

All buildings receive solar energy and the idea of using it more effectively is not new. However, the application of passive solar concepts to schools is relatively recent. The following pages give a brief historical background to passive solar design in schools.

This bulletin does not consider **active** solar systems, such as solar energy (i.e. heat) collector panels and photovoltaic panels, because there are very few examples of their use in schools in the UK and the technologies are still developing.

Chapter 1 Historical background

During the 19th century and up until the turn of the century, schools were predominantly designed to take advantage of northlight and so glare from south or west facing windows was avoided.

19th century school design using northlight. Northern facade of Henderson Avenue School, Crosby, Lancashire.

Interior view of same school

From 1900 up to the 1930s, there was an increase in awareness of the importance of fresh air and sunlight to health. This led to the open-air school movement. Schools were oriented in a southerly direction and could employ folding or sliding windows so that teaching areas were exposed to fresh air and direct sunlight for at least some hours during the day.

A 1930s open-air school with windows which fold back

In the 1940s, the importance of facilitating sunlight penetration into classrooms was restated and a minimum 2% daylight 'sky factor' was introduced in 1945 with a memorandum recommending 5% where possible. ('Sky factor' was more demanding than the daylight factor we now use). Hence many schools were constructed in the 1950s and 1960s with highly glazed facades. Unfortunately many of these school buildings were thermally inefficient lightweight structures which overheated uncontrollably during summer and suffered high rates of heat loss in winter. Early system-built schools were particularly prone to these adverse effects.

The first passive solar school in the UK, St Mary's in Wallasey, was built in 1961. This is the only example of a school with no heating system. All heat was provided by solar gain, occupancy gains and by tungsten lights. However some occupants of the school complained of stuffiness.

The oil price crises in the 1970s brought about the development of more energy efficient schools and renewed interest in passive-solar design. Since the early 1980s, a number of schools with passive solar features have been built, some of which are included in this study.

During the last 25 years, because of improved energy efficiency and other reasons (e.g. better lighting spectra), fluorescent lighting has been almost universally adopted in schools. Also, the discipline of daylight planning was often neglected as schools were planned to rely on electric light. Energy efficiency measures concentrated on reducing heat losses by building designs with compact plan forms, small window areas, and increased fabric insulation. As a consequence electric lighting demands formed a significant proportion of the total energy consumption.

Classic cross-section of the 1940s to maximise daylight

St Mary's, Wallasey

Reduced window area and dark floor colour produce a reliance on electric lighting

By contrast a good passive solar design would make much more effective use of ambient daylight thus reducing electricity consumption. Passive solar design involves the optimal balance of maximising daylight and utilising solar energy whilst excluding glare and avoiding overheating. While passive solar design is a relatively new concept, emphasis on good environmental conditions has been a preoccupation of school designers for a long time.

Chapter 2 Basic principles

2.1. Introduction

All buildings, as they are exposed to the ambient environment, interact to a varying extent with the local climate. The design and siting of a building, or group of buildings, has a significant effect on this interaction, and implicit in the design of a passive solar building is the wish to maximise the benefits of ambient energy from the sun.

This naturally available energy can be used to augment the heating, lighting and ventilation of such a building, in order to produce acceptable levels of comfort. If the principles of passive solar design are successfully applied, the result should be an amply lit building, with an energy consumption lower than that of a building of conventional design.

To achieve the improved utilisation of solar energy inherent in this design concept, elements of the building are used to collect, store and distribute solar energy in such a way that fuel bills are reduced. The building elements are also designed to protect the occupants from unwanted solar gains, which would otherwise cause overheating or discomfort.

Whenever the use of solar energy is to be optimised in a building, the design of its built form, fabric, windows, services systems and controls, must be considered in an integrated manner, having due regard to the site, its orientation and local microclimate. The function and patterns of use of the building also need to be considered and most importantly the comfort requirements should be addressed.

This chapter looks at the design strategy it is recommended should be adopted for developing a passive solar building, and then looks at all the design factors. Finally, the last part of the chapter considers computer simulation exercises of the thermal behaviour of buildings and draws some design guidance from them.

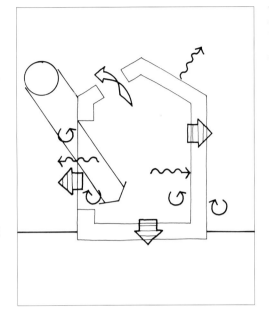

All buildings, as they are exposed to the external environment, interact to varying extents with the local climate. Heat transfer mechanisms, including conduction, convection, radiation and evaporation will occur.

2.2. Design strategy

It is only possible to get a good passive solar school building through the application of a design philosophy which respects the climate, the surrounding external environment, and allows the designer to select those environmental elements which best compliment the nature, use, and occupancy of the building, whilst filtering out those of a less desirable nature.

Many would simply view this approach as 'good design', because, if proper regard is not given to the aesthetic, environmental and technical considerations for a new building or when designing refurbishment proposals, then the result is likely to be a less than satisfactory building.

Sadly in many developments all the factors are not considered adequately in an inter-related way during the design stage and so the resulting buildings leave a lot to be desired.

A retrospective process of simply adding passive solar features as an afterthought, such as sun spaces or roof space collectors, either to a completed design, or an existing building, without such consideration, might well result in a solution which is wasteful and unnecessarily expensive. There may also be an increased risk of daytime

Basic principles

A fundamental aspect of successful passive solar design is the use and control of solar gain and daylight. Without due consideration, such factors as glare can become a distracting or even disabling problem at certain times during the school day.

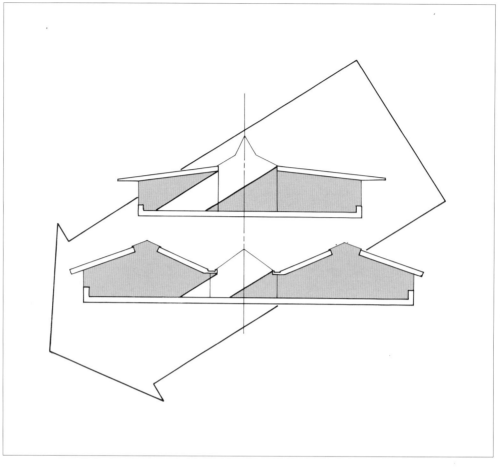

Gains from occupancy, equipment and solar energy all affect the comfort of the occupants.

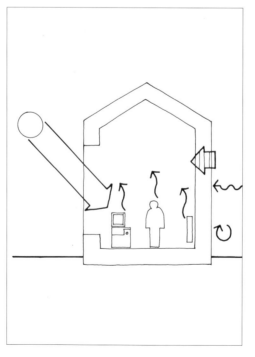

overheating compared with that for a more conventional design.

A fundamental aspect of passive solar design is the successful use and control of solar gain, daylight, and natural ventilation.

The heating, ventilation, lighting systems and controls, have essential roles to play: the internal environment can be seriously disturbed by solar gain being admitted if due attention is not given to its effects.

Any overall strategy involving passive solar design must include an appreciation of both the climate and the performance of the building throughout the year, because features which enhance solar gain in the winter heating season may in turn create overheating problems during the summer and autumn.

The factors which should play major parts in the design of passive solar schools are now considered.

2.3 Human comfort

In any passive solar building, the comfort of the occupants is of paramount importance: it is very easy to make design errors leading to a lack of ventilation and overheating.

Thermal comfort occurs when an individual is in a state of physical and mental well-being. For the occupants of a building, comfort conditions are usually assessed on the needs of a group rather than those of an individual. Thermal comfort can however be defined as the condition under which an individual desires neither a warmer nor a colder environment.

The factors influencing indoor thermal comfort are firstly personal matters, such as activity and clothing, and secondly the environmental conditions, such as air temperature, air velocity and humidity. This second group is dependent on the design of the building.

Gains from occupancy, equipment use and solar energy can all affect whether or not comfort conditions are achieved.

Solar gains need to be controlled, and this is usually accomplished by shading, using overhanging eaves, some form of fixed or moveable shades, blinds, or deciduous vegetation.

2.4 Climate and microclimate

Good design takes account of the effects of the climate on the internal environment of a building. A series of quantifiable regional climatic factors, such as intensity of solar radiation, temperature, humidity and wind speed, are necessary to establish the relationship between the external environment and the requirements of a building for heating, ventilation and/or cooling.

It is important to consider changes in local conditions, especially the micro-climate at the site. Topography and water are two examples of the surface geography of the land which can affect the microclimate. Soil, vegetation and urban density can also be important factors

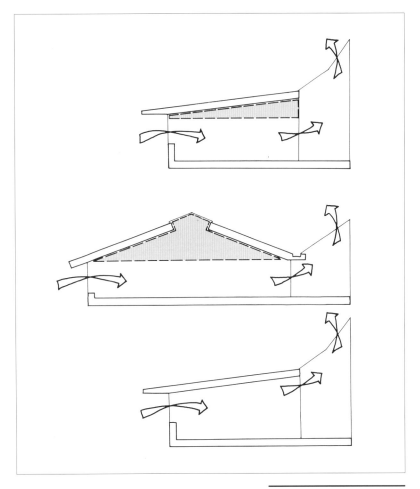

affecting the local climate.

An assessment of local climatic conditions should always be part of the initial site appraisal, to be carried out before consideration can be given to the form which a passive solar building should take.

2.5 Direct gain

When solar radiation enters a room through glazed windows or roof lights, it is partly absorbed or reflected within the space. The resultant temperature rise is referred to as direct gain.

In the United Kingdom glazed apertures should face south, or within 30 degrees of due south and be vertical or near vertical for good winter performance in terms of achieving a high direct gain from solar radiation.

Direct gain appears to be the most common method for harnessing solar

Errors in passive solar design can lead to a lack of ventilation and overheating. Even with cross ventilation, induced by the stack effect in the attached atria, the roof configuration and position of vents of the first two examples above lead to warm air being trapped just above head height. The third design, although similar to the first, is intended to take advantage of natural convection, thus venting the warm air away from the occupants.

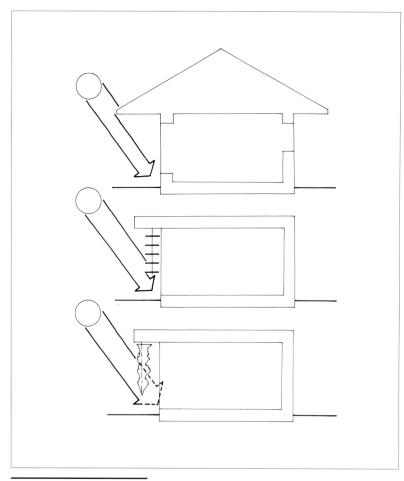

Shading can be used to control the amount of solar gain to a building. This can be done using overhanging eaves, blinds or deciduous vegetation.

The design of windows has to be carefully considered to avoid discomfort. Direct insolation of a large area of a room and its occupants can occur. Asymmetrical heating or cooling of occupants close to windows can also lead to discomfort.

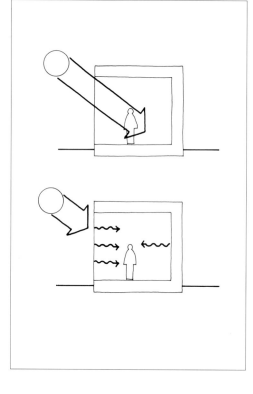

energy in school buildings, despite the problems of glare and overheating which are often associated with it. Many examples exist of unsatisfactory designs in this respect.

The effective use of direct gain presents particular challenges to the designers of school buildings. These may include:

(a) direct insolation(i.e. direct as opposed to diffuse sunlight) of a large area of the room and its occupants;

(b) visual disability and discomfort due to problems of glare;

(c) damage to fabrics and finishes from exposure to the ultra-violet radiation of the solar spectrum, and

(d) summertime overheating.

Providing these design challenges are met and solved, the main advantages of adopting a direct gain approach include incurring little or no extra cost and a simple and virtually self-functioning operation. However, extreme care needs to be devoted to the pattern of fenestration chosen, and design of windows and opening lights.

2.6 Windows

The use of appropriately oriented windows is the most obvious method of capturing solar radiation in a room. Orientation can be used to optimise this gain which will occur at any angle from east to west through south.

In such a direct gain room the mechanism of heat transfer is principally radiative between the surfaces of the room. If there is sufficient thermal mass in the room, heat is absorbed and stored for a period of hours. This has the effect of minimising temperature fluctuations and may avoid excessive temperatures arising during periods of high insolation.

North facing windows gain little advantage from solar radiation in terms of heat, and may be a significant source of heat loss, but they are useful for admitting daylight from diffuse radiation, providing heat losses can be reduced by the use of double glazing or translucent insulation.

The ratio of window to wall areas is important in determining the energy consumption of a building. As the window size increases, so does the rate of heat loss, but there are energy benefits from increased solar gain and daylight. In any design, these conflicting factors need to be carefully considered.

For comfort conditions within a building with non south facing windows, the calculated primary-energy consumption varies by only 5% if the glazing is between 20 and 40% of the internal area of the external wall, but when the glazing area exceeds 40%, the energy requirement rises significantly, whereas below 20% there is no corresponding saving in energy. It is therefore recommended to use between 20% and 40% glazing on non south facing elevations.

2.7 Shading

Ideally shading devices should reduce direct solar radiation whilst admitting diffuse radiation as daylight. This selective mode of radiation control is difficult to attain, because all shading devices reduce daylight availability.

External shading devices provide very effective shading, because the solar energy is rejected before it can enter the building. However they tend to be expensive, due to the need for weather resistance.

Different types of shading device may be equally effective in reducing solar gain, but have a varying influence on the view obtained through a window.

Fixed or movable external shading devices can be successful in reducing unwanted solar gains and the associated instances of glare, but, even when shading is present, there may be times when direct sunlight is likely to cause problems of glare, and so internal blinds become essential.

Fixed shading devices depend on the seasonal geometry of the angle of incidence of the direct solar radiation to permit some selective control of solar radiation to be achieved. However attention must be given to the orientation, inclination and the geometry of fixed overhangs and fins. An important advantage of fixed shading devices is that they are 'passive' or self operating. However they must be of robust design to avoid damage from snow loading, and the effect on window cleaning operations has to be considered. The lightweight external fixed shading on at least one school was damaged by a combination of snow loading and the unfortunate attentions of the pupils.

The addition of large overhangs above windows results in a reduction of the average daylight factor in rooms, but can reduce the high levels of light and glare in the vicinity of large windows.

However, a horizontal overhang of one metre at lintel height will completely shade a two-metre-high window in mid-summer; about 10% of it in midwinter; and almost 50% in the spring, when the

An overhang will provide different amounts of shade according to the season of the year.
Depending on the size and position of the overhang complete shading can be achieved in midsummer. In midwinter only a small amount of shade is afforded by the same overhang.

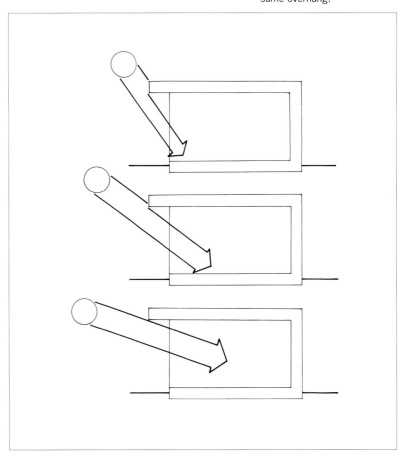

direct gain and extra daylight would be most useful in shortening the heating season, and obviating the need for electric lighting. The use of such shading devices in deep plan school buildings could result in the need for permanent artificial lighting, which would be undesirable.

Moveable shading devices are more responsive, although their movement mechanisms can present installation and maintenance problems. The weather has control implications for some devices, such as awnings, which must be withdrawn if the wind is strong. External blinds have, however, been used extensively and successfully in Southern Europe.

Interior and exterior light shelves can be incorporated in the fenestration to provide:

(a) external shading, which reduces summertime overheating, and

(b) improved daylight distribution, which reduces the glare in rooms by masking a direct view of the sky, reducing the brightness of surfaces exposed to direct daylight and areas near the windows.

A lightshelf can be incorporated in the fenestration design to provide both shading and improved daylight distribution within the room

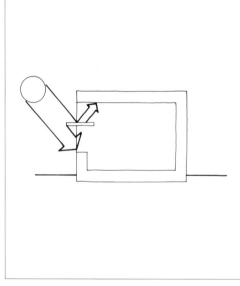

Indoor shading devices attempt to block the solar radiation which has already passed through the glazing. A component of the radiation which has been blocked in this way is reflected back by the glazing, and radiation is absorbed by the surface of the shading device, which, although shielding the occupants from the worst effects of direct solar radiation, becomes a radiant heat source and can contribute to overheating within the building.

2.8 Thermal mass

During winter, the heating system in a passive solar building must respond quickly to provide heat to a particular zone when useful solar gains cease, and regulate the emission of heat to allow for the variable level of solar gains, when they resume.

The high thermal mass of a direct gain building also tends to ameliorate the immediate effects of solar gains, and helps provide more stable classroom temperatures.

Three categories of thermal mass can be identified in direct gain systems:

(a) Primary mass, being that of the internal walls and floor surfaces which are exposed to the sun-patch in a classroom, and which are thereby directly insolated. For United Kingdom latitudes, the diurnal sun-patch movement constrains the location of primary mass to either the floor or lower areas of the internal walls. Unfortunately this is often undesirable, as these areas should be available for use by the pupils. Thus provision of primary mass is difficult without resorting to fixed masonry window benches, and in any case the surfaces of these will, in practice, be covered.

(b) Secondary mass is that which is insolated by diffuse and reflected short-wave radiation and long-wave thermal radiation from directly insolated, primary mass surfaces. Secondary mass is more available than primary mass, because it is provided by the ceilings and unobstructed upper surfaces of internal walls, which are less effective for storage than primary mass, as they are often of lightweight construction. However, in winter, when heating is required, the diffuse component of the insolation and the reflected radiation received by the secondary mass can be greater than the available direct insolation.

(c) Tertiary mass is that located in a zone not receiving directly any solar gains. Instead it gains heat from air warmed and transferred from the direct gain space by convection or mechanical ventilation. To make effective use of tertiary mass, door openings, grilles, or fans and purpose-made ducts must be incorporated into the design.

The greater the thermal mass of a direct gain school building, the lower and later in the day will be the peak internal temperature attained in a classroom exposed to prolonged periods of high solar gain, with consequently fewer complaints from pupils and teachers. Conventional masonry or timber framed construction can be used, in most circumstances, to provide an adequate constructional thermal mass. The effective thermal mass (for this purpose) of a dense concrete wall does not increase significantly once its thickness exceeds 0.1 metre typically.

Internal partitions can absorb heat more rapidly than the inner surfaces of external walls, because the former usually have two air-contacting surfaces with which to gain heat from the internal environment. Thus plasterboard partitions, though regarded as lightweight in terms of construction, can provide an important contribution to the required thermal mass, particularly if the plasterboard partition is of double layered, double skin construction.

It is usual for new or refurbished classrooms to have carpet on the floor, and for the interior walls to be lined to some extent with pin boards, possibly to door head height for display purposes. These materials have the effect of low thermal mass, even when applied to concrete surfaces, causing solar gains to have a more immediate effect on room temperature than might be desirable.

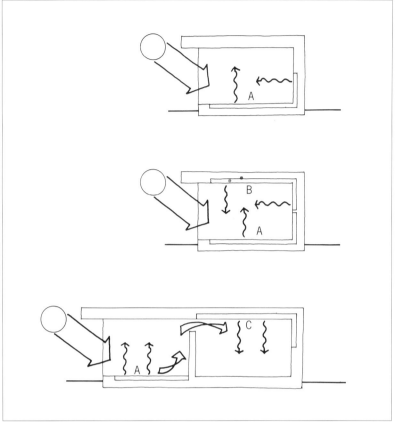

The amount of thermal mass that is available also has implications for the control and pre-heating of the internal environment.

The three categories of thermal mass include:

A   Primary mass
B   Secondary mass
C   Tertiary mass

2.9 Overheating

As thermal insulation standards have improved, there is a greater risk of potential overheating from direct solar gain in buildings. Internal occupancy gains have changed little in the last twenty years, but internal equipment gains have increased with the greater use of information technology. Solar gain therefore can be a critical factor in the potential for a building to overheat at certain times of the school year.

The model of a simple school building used to test various design options with respect to thermal performance and daylighting

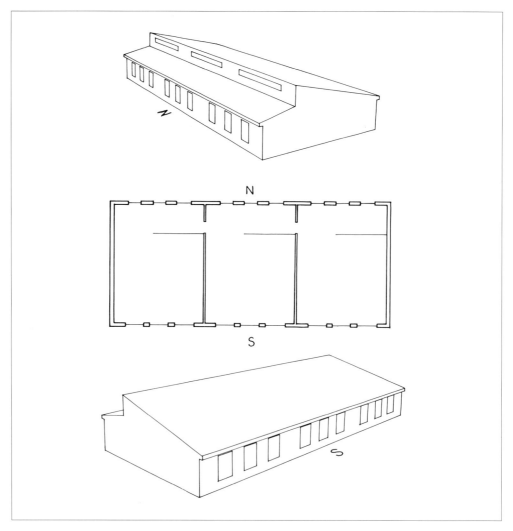

2.10 Testing of design options

As a part of this study Cranfield University carried out computer simulations to compare effects of various design options.

A model of a simple school building of three class-bases with associated activity spaces and circulation areas was used.

Commonly adopted insulation and construction standards having the following U-values were assumed:

roofs and walls	0.25 W/m²K
floor	0.45 W/m²K
windows	2.80 W/m²K

A system of mono-pitched roofs was modelled to test for heat build-up due to the lack of a buffer effect of a normal pitched roof void and to allow for clerestory glazing and cross ventilation of the class-base. The space was 10.5 metres deep, and lit from both sides. A constant fenestration area of 20% of the internal face of the external wall area was used for the activity spaces and the clerestory glazing to the class-bases.

The main glazing of the class-base was varied between 20% and 40% of the internal face of the external wall. Eaves-level projections of 300 mm were assumed as standard throughout, with a variation modelled to show the effect of 600 mm and 900 mm projections on the south facade.

Daylight factors and uniformity ratios were predicted. [The uniformity ratio is the minimum daylight factor divided by the average daylight factor in a space.]

The results shown on the next page suggest that eaves overhangs of greater than 300 mm do not produce a significant benefit for the substantial additional cost incurred.

Primary school class-base with associated activity space and circulation area.

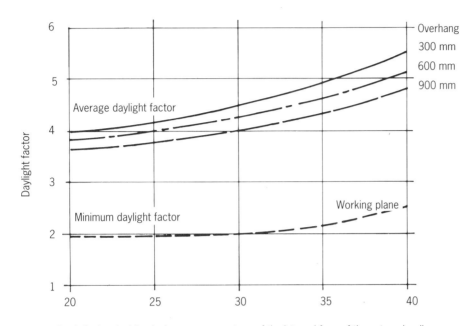

South facing double glazing as a percentage of the internal face of the external wall

Daylight factors were predicted for increasing percentages of south facing double glazing and increasingly deep overhangs. Note also the minimum daylight factor at the working plane.

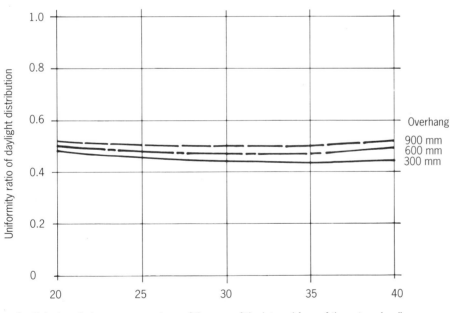

South facing glazing as a percentage of the area of the internal face of the external wall

Uniformity ratio of daylight distribution for increasing percentages of south facing double glazing and increasingly deep overhangs.

Assumes 20% of the internal face of the North wall is double glazed
South facing shading projection at 2.4 m above finished floor level

The hours of 'lamp on' for increasing percentages of south facing double glazing and increasingly deep overhangs

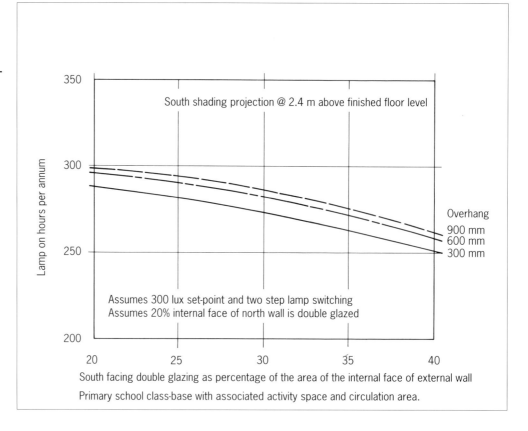

Electric lighting periods and associated electric loads were also modelled assuming that all use of electric lighting was sensitive to the availability of daylight. This is governed by a set-point level of 300 lux, and switched in two equal steps, which is the optimal arrangement, if somewhat unrealistic in practice. The results for a single class-base and activity space situation are shown.

The kWh electric lighting per annum for increasing percentages of south facing double glazing and increasingly deep overhangs

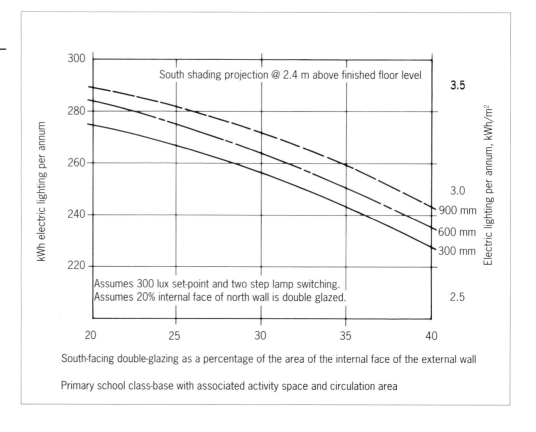

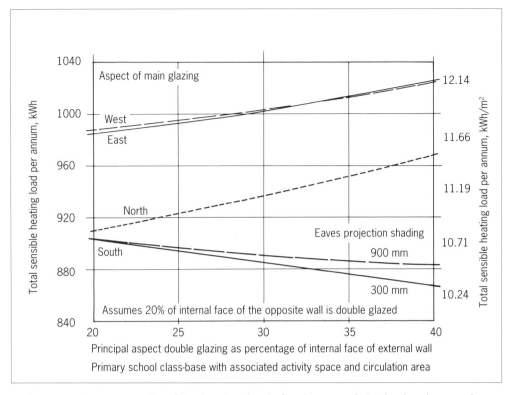

The heating loads for different orientations of main glazing. Note. The variation with the eaves' projection is shown only for the southerly aspect class-base. Given this configuration of building form and glazing specification, the north-south orientation performs better than the east-west aspect.

A comparison was made of the heating loads for the central single class-base and activity space to show the effect of different orientations, and the effect of large eaves' projections on a southerly aspect class-base.

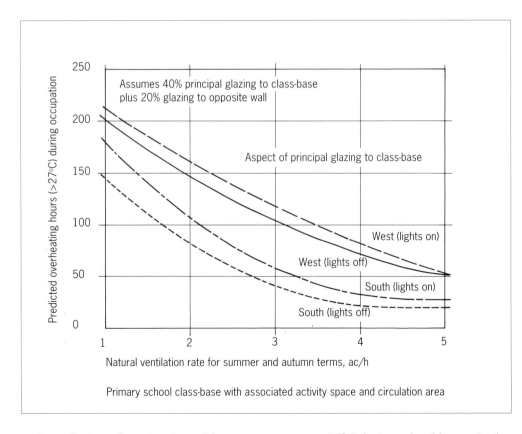

The predicted overheating hours during occupation, with and without lights on, with varying natural ventilation rates for southerly and westerly aspects.

A prediction of overheating with temperatures over 27°C during school hours, in the summer and autumn terms, for a class-base with main aspect glazing of 40% is shown.

The predicted overheating days for increasing percentages of south aspect double glazing.

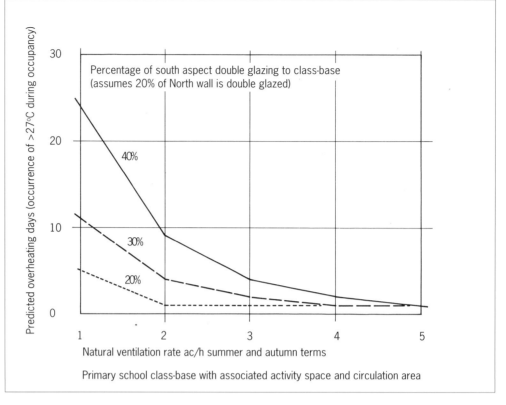

The number of days of overheating was predicted for southerly aspect glazing of 20%, 30% and 40% fenestration in relation to varying natural ventilation rates. A 300 mm eaves' projection with the sensible use of blinds and the lights off were the parameters chosen. The results clearly show the importance of achieving good natural ventilation which is draught free. Many schools with large areas of glass do not have window designs which permit this and therefore suffer from overheating.

2.11   Achieving a balance

The incorporation of passive solar features in a building can be either advantageous or problematic, depending on the design approach taken.   The interaction of solar gain with the functions of the building can either enhance its performance, or lead to overheating and the resultant discomfort of the occupants.

Various interactions, inherent in passive solar design, can have many consequences in the finished building.   Therefore it is necessary to take extreme care when adopting this design strategy, to make sure that the right decisions about the solar features to be included are taken at appropriate stages in the development and evaluation of a design.

The right decisions will be made if passive solar features are included on the basis that they complement not only the use of the building, but also its form, location, microclimate and environmental requirements.

A successful passive solar school will not only be a pleasant building in which to work, but will also have a relatively low rate of energy consumption.

Chapter 3 Features and components

Although an integrated design process is required to produce the truly climate sensitive design solution inherent in the passive solar concept, it is useful to discuss separately some of the major features found in passive solar design solutions.

3.1.1 Atria

In recent years atria have become familiar elements of buildings. They are very popular in new buildings, and in schemes where the refurbishment and remodelling of older buildings is undertaken. Their advantage in retrofitting is that the space between two or more separate buildings can be covered by a glazed atrium roof to provide additional usable space at relatively low extra cost, and without having to make major alterations to the adjoining accommodation.

Where young children are being taught such areas often form an integral part of the school. Practical work, reading and displays can all be located in an atrium.

In a secondary school, where perhaps a glazed street has been included, the space gained, though used for educational activities, may be considered more important as a social area for pupils. During inclement weather, and when not under instruction, adolescents in these areas can be supervised with fewer staff than would be required if the students stayed in their classrooms.

It is often assumed that the inclusion of an atrium in a building will result in energy savings, but this is not always so. Unless carefully designed, such a feature may turn out to be extremely wasteful of energy. A retrofitted atrium may significantly reduce the level of daylight received or natural ventilation to the surrounding rooms, and result in additional lighting and mechanical ventilation being required so that the advantages of the atrium are lost.

However sun-spaces, if correctly designed, can provide:

(a) daylight to adjacent spaces;

(b) ventilation from adjacent spaces in hot weather and tempered ventilation to adjacent spaces during cold weather;

(c) a useful space with a comfortable environment;

(d) a buffer zone between the inside and ambient environments, and

(e) a saving in heating energy by virtue of their ability to capture and utilise solar energy.

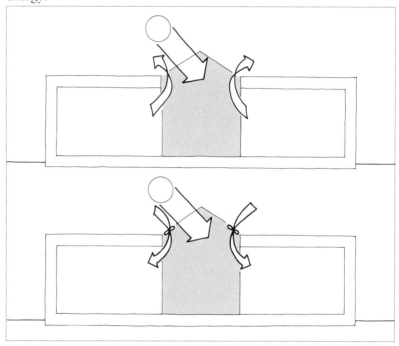

An atrium can provide ventilation from adjacent spaces in hot weather and tempered ventilation to adjacent spaces in cold weather

3.1.2 Types of atria

There are two common forms found in schools, namely:
°   the courtyard atrium
°   the linear central atrium

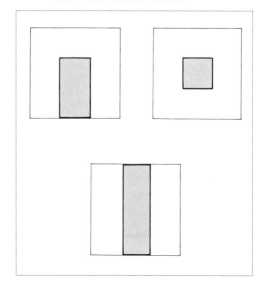

Typical forms of atria found in schools include the courtyard atrium which can either be open or closed and the linear or 'street' atrium

The courtyard atrium

This form, in which a glazed roof is added to cover a space between buildings, can be especially useful in lowering the energy consumption of a school, providing the connection between the atrium and the adjoining spaces is designed to allow sufficient light and natural ventilation to the adjacent spaces. The advantages are that this atrium can reduce the overall perimeter of the building exposed to the ambient environment, and provide a buffer space between the inside and outside.   A fully-enclosed atrium requires minimal heating as a circulation area in winter, because heat gains from adjacent spaces and solar gains will generally be sufficient to maintain adequate temperatures.

The linear central atrium

Formed between two blocks of accommodation so heat losses from the ends are comparatively high and some heating is more likely to be required if full utilisation of the space is demandèd.

3.1.3 Heated or unheated

Atria can be either heated or unheated, although in the latter case an atrium may be unusable for certain periods during the winter. The decision to include heating may be dictated solely by financial considerations or by the ultimate use to which the atrium is to be put. Whether or not an atrium is heated, it is essential to provide for a considerable area of high level openings for ventilation to reduce the summertime tendency to overheat.

Unheated atria have been used in primary schools to provide circulation space and extra occasional space for practical work, when conditions in the atrium are suitable. Heated atria have also been used for these purposes, but more usually they form part of the basic teaching area of schools and can contain shared resources such as libraries. Barnes Farm infants school is an example of a school with an unheated atrium.

However, the space is so popular with the staff that they would have preferred it to have been heated to allow use throughout the year. This suggests that whilst atria which are intended to be used principally as circulation spaces need not be heated directly, an intermittently occupied atrium may need some additional heating system. In such cases, overhead radiant heating might be appropriate for cold days to compensate for radiant losses to the cold glass, which avoids the need to heat the whole air mass by convection and associated high conduction losses through the glass. Where atria are heated the heat loss should be minimised. This can be done by using double glazing and by not glazing the entire structure. The roof and walls need not be fully glazed.

An atrium can reduce the energy consumption of a school by the natural or forced circulation of warmer than ambient air between the atrium and the building, and by reducing the area of the walls of the main accommodation which are exposed to cold ambient conditions.

At first sight, it would appear that an atrium which is heated, would result in a net energy loss from the building. However this may not necessarily be the case. The energy balance will depend on the conductance of the glazing, the shape of the structure, the heating regime, occupancy patterns and other factors.

3.1.4 Daylighting

The warmer than ambient environment of an atrium makes it possible to increase the area of windows facing into it.   In addition, the reduced levels of daylight availability in an atrium, compared with the exterior, mean that the windows between the atrium and adjoining spaces should always be made as large as possible to maximise the daylight availability in the adjacent teaching spaces, otherwise daylight levels in them might be too low.

3.1.5 Monitored examples

Having examined the design of atria in both newly built and refurbished schools, two examples of school atria are now discussed. Both examples are for infant schools located in southeast England, and their details are referred to in the case studies.

Briefly, both schools are of single storey construction, and have class-bases located either side of a central atrium, which provides both accommodation and a link with the other spaces in each school. Barnes Farm Infants School was purpose built with an unheated atrium providing relatively low cost extra space, which is usable for most, but not quite all, of the school year.

The other school, Hook Infants, was remodelled and extended to incorporate a new heated atrium, which is used as a teaching area, and intended to be used throughout the year. Both atria provide delightful well lit spaces, which are much

appreciated, but overheating can be a problem.

The usefulness of the unheated atrium space at Barnes Farm on a cool winter's day with some sunshine, is illustrated below.

The monitored information shows that the space usually meets comfort requirements during the period of occupancy. However, this unheated atrium would be unusable for teaching purposes due to being uncomfortable on some winter days, totalling about one month each winter.

Ventilation

Atria must always be provided with adequate and reliable means for venting excess heat. In both schools, opening lights were incorporated in the atrium roof.

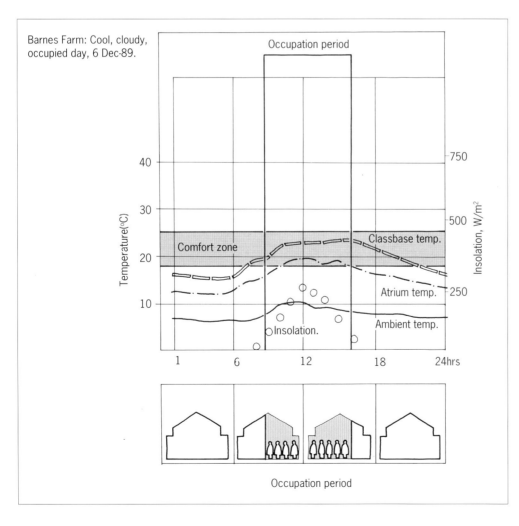

Barnes Farm: Cool, cloudy, occupied day, 6 Dec-89.

A graphical representation of the thermal performance of the unheated atrium space at Barnes Farm School on a cool winter's day. The monitored information shows that the space meets comfort requirements during the period of occupancy.

A graphical representation of the thermal performance of the atrium at Barnes Farm School on a hot and sunny day. Although the atrium had overheated before vents were opened, the internal temperature of the atrium quickly dropped to almost that of the ambient environment, once the vents were opened.

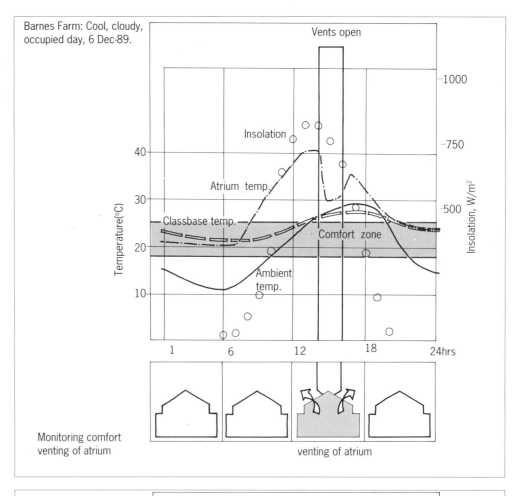

Barnes Farm: Cool, cloudy, occupied day, 6 Dec-89.

A graphical representation of the thermal performance of the atrium at Hook School on a hot and sunny day. The opening of the vents has a negligible effect on the internal temperature of the atrium which prior to the opening of the vents had overheated.

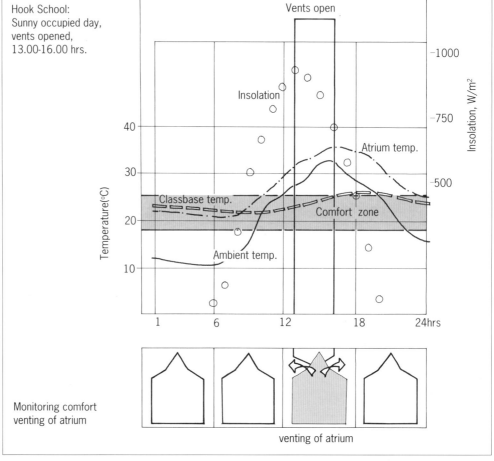

Hook School:
Sunny occupied day,
vents opened,
13.00-16.00 hrs.

In the unheated new build design at Barnes Farm, approximately one third of the glazed roof area was openable at ridge height using a reliable, motorised rack and pinion mechanism to open the ridge vents. This was set to manual control during the monitoring period, but could operate automatically if required. The effectiveness of this arrangement of roof vents for natural ventilation of atria to control summertime overheating is evident from the monitoring information for the typically hot and sunny day, as illustrated opposite. During the period of occupancy, the atrium was allowed to overheat considerably before the roof vents were opened. The internal temperature of the atrium quickly dropped, almost to ambient temperature once the vents were opened.

Computer simulation and monitoring of Barnes Farm showed the benefit of automatic control of roof ventilation in shared spaces. This is because the occupants tend to delay opening the vents whereas an automatic system can be set to open the vents early and thereby prevent the overheating taking place. However manual over-ride control will be necessary to allow for sudden changes in weather.

A much smaller proportion of the atrium roof area of the remodelled Hook Infants' School was openable using top-hung roof vents unfortunately with unreliable cord-operated gearing. The lack of effectiveness of the arrangement, with only about four per cent of the glazed roof openable, is shown on the opposite page. Once more the atrium overheated before the roof vents were opened, but in this case the opening of the available vents had a negligible effect on the mean atrium temperature.

Fire ventilation

There are two reasons for ventilation. The first is to cool the space and prevent summertime overheating. The second only applies in atria of two storeys or higher. This is ventilation in case of fire and can be used as an alternative to providing enclosed staircases. Fire ventilation must be carefully engineered and computerised fluid dynamics smoke movement analyses are often used. The resulting fire vents and smoke extract mechanisms can also be used to provide summertime ventilation if thermostatically controlled (see Swanlea case study).

Computer simulation

Several aspects of both of the atria designs and their consequences were examined, based on the results of dynamic thermal simulation, and an associated parametric analysis of the thermal behaviour of the two schools. The results concerning dependance on orientation and atrium-width are of some interest.

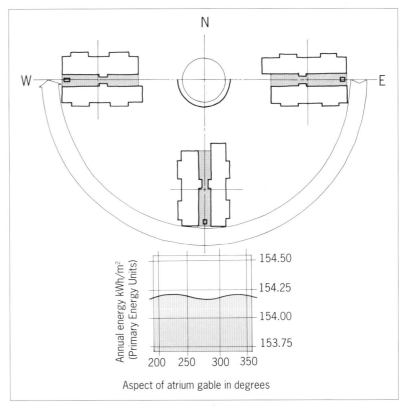

Orientation

In order to study the effect of orientation on the thermal performance of these primary school buildings with central atria, changes in the orientation of both buildings were simulated in steps of 15 degrees, using a computer model. An annual run of hourly data was used to predict the resultant annual energy demand for each change of orientation of the otherwise 'as constructed' building.

In both cases as illustrated above there

The graph shows that orientation has a negligible effect on the thermal performance of these primary schools with central atria was a negligible effect predicted for changing the orientation of the schools.

This is because the major part of the useful solar gain to the building is via incidence on the atria from above.   The axial orientation of the atrium is unlikely to affect this gain significantly, and the atrium gain dominates the effect of changing the aspect of the remaining fenestration to the building. This would seem to indicate that this form of school building, with a central atrium, could be used advantageously on sites where a southerly orientation of the building is impractical.

Construction of atria

Atria roof glazing should always be double glazed to avoid overnight condensation problems and where an atrium is heated the end walls should be double glazed.

To avoid summertime overheating it is best to incorporate considerable thermal mass into an atrium. At Barnes Farm this is achieved by using brick walls between the classrooms and the atrium and by using a heavyweight tiled floor. In contrast the floor at Hook is covered by carpet. However the overheating at Hook is mainly due to the inadequate size of the roof vents. Opaque areas of roof or wall and external shades also reduce solar heat-gain. The roof does not need to be fully glazed. The roof at Hook Infants is not glazed on the south side to limit both heat loss and heat gain.

Width of a central atrium

The Barnes Farm School is built of heavyweight construction with an unheated atrium of 6.2 metres width, and the Hook School is of relatively lightweight construction with a 5.5 metres-wide heated atrium.

The computer simulations for Barnes Farm predicted that overheating would become critical for widths of atrium exceeding 7 metres.

The equivalent results for the heated atrium of the Hook School type of construction predict the problem of overheating revealed in the monitored data, and indicate that it increases with the width of atrium.The principal reasons for the overheating are the lack of thermal mass in the lightweight steel structure and the inadequate area of roof vents.

When an atrium is heated the heat loss also increases with width which is a further reason to limit the width.

As a general rule single storey atria should not be more than 7 metres wide. The lower limit on the width of an atrium is largely determined by space utilisation.

3.2 Conservatories.

A conservatory is an enclosed space with a glazed roof and one or more glass walls attached to the side of a building. Normally a conservatory will be attached to the south side of a building to harness direct or indirect solar gain. Conservatories provide a useful physical, thermal and visual buffer space between the internal and external environments. For these reasons they are popular features in both new build and retrofit applications.

3.2.1 Operation of conservatories

Conservatories function in a number of ways to heat or cool a space.

As a buffer zone, the conservatory provides an additional thermal resistance to the attached side of the building, so reducing overall heat losses providing a traditional heating system is not used in the conservatory.

If the classrooms are situated on the northern side of a school, a south facing conservatory can be added as an unheated corridor or circulation space. This releases extra space inside the school for teaching purposes.

Solar gains captured by the conservatory can be transferred to the adjacent rooms by natural convection. However for a significant transfer of heat to occur, there must be a sufficient temperature difference between the conservatory and the adjacent rooms. This can result in the temperature of the conservatory becoming uncomfortably high.

In the cooling mode, the egress of hot air at high level as a result of the stack effect may allow cooling of not only the conservatory, but also the adjacent rooms. This requires sufficient height within a conservatory with high level vents, and suitable openings between the conservatory and the adjoining spaces.

3.2.2 Types of conservatory

Conservatories can be divided into three types:-

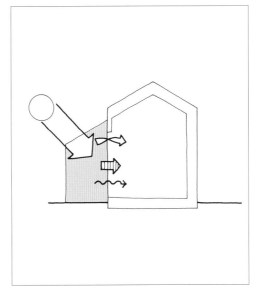

Integral direct: these are coupled to the classrooms via a glazed lightweight partition. This partition will usually allow infiltration of air to occur between its two sides. Heat gains to the building are by natural ventilation, direct radiative gain, conduction and by a reduction of the heat loss via facades abutting the conservatory.

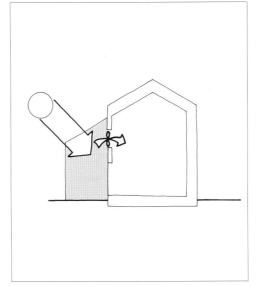

Integral indirect: here the glazed area of the separating partition is usually smaller and the contribution of direct radiative gain is reduced compared with that for an integral direct system. The fabric of the partition is less susceptible to air infiltration, and ventilation with solar pre-heated air is usually accomplished mechanically. There is more opportunity to isolate the conservatory from the main body of the school.

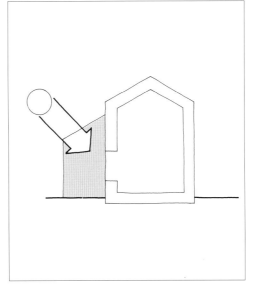

Attached isolated: in this system, the relative glazed area is also small, and the separating partition is usually of external wall construction, probably with insulation. This category includes retrofitted glazed areas and streets.

3.2.3 Natural ventilation

Passive solar buildings with conservatories often rely ultimately upon air movement to provide the heat transfer. Airflow and infiltration through buildings are both dependent upon several factors. These include the wind's speed and direction, the temperature difference between the building and the ambient environment and the aerodynamic form of the building. In addition, the overall air-tightness of the building, in regard to the type and position of its openings, will be a factor as will the surrounding topography and obstructions. The designer should try to use these effects to optimise the air flow for a maximum pre-heating effect.

Where the permeability of the building and wind direction are favourable, conservatories can reduce ventilation heat-loads by pre-heating the air which subsequently passes to the rest of the building. The air flows are induced by the temperature difference between the warm conservatory and the cooler adjacent classrooms.

This mode of operation of a conservatory carries the important advantage that all solar gains provide some reduction of the ventilation heat load, which constitutes a large proportion of the annual energy consumption in school buildings. In addition, as schools become better insulated generally, so the proportion of energy that is used to heat the air will increase.

However, it should be remembered that in northern European climates, only low air flow rates ensue for the small temperature differences encountered typically in spring or autumn: thus energy transport is minimal. In summer, such action needs to be prevented in order to avoid overheating.

Many examples of conservatories examined did not perform well thermally, and the spaces provided often overheated and so were not particularly useful. In shallow-plan, multiple-storey buildings, wind driven infiltration may distribute solar heat from conservatories effectively. However the deep plans of many single-storey UK primary schools do not facilitate the use of ventilation and air movement to distribute pre-heated ventilation air from a conservatory unless the conservatory is properly designed to achieve this.

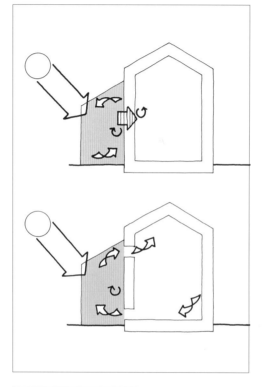

Solar gains captured by the conservatory can be transferred to the adjacent rooms.

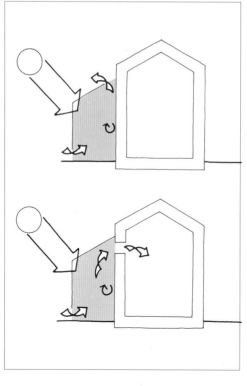

The egress of hot air at high level through the stack effect may allow cooling of not only the conservatory, but also adjacent rooms.

Fresh air is pre-heated in the conservatory and carried into the building by natural convection.

3.2.4 Forced ventilation

Natural circulation of air between the conservatory and the heated building occurs when windows or doors open into the conservatory.

In some cases, provision is made for ducts and fans to facilitate the air flow.

Where ducts are used, 'flap valves' have to be provided to prevent nocturnal and winter reverse flow occuring when the temperature in the conservatory is less than in the heated building. However, a contribution to a lower heat load still ensues from the reduction in the rate of thermal conduction through the separating wall.

In well insulated buildings with short heating seasons, temperatures in an attached conservatory are above internal temperatures only rarely. Hence the annual heating contribution is likely to be small. This has to be considered carefully when assessing the economics of the energy gained against the energy consumed by the fan used to produce the forced circulation of air between the conservatory and the building.

3.2.5 Thermal mass

One advantage of using passive solar principles in school design is that heating is required in such buildings mostly during daylight hours. Extensive and costly heat storage is therefore not necessary. If energy storage were considered desirable, it would be necessary to store the heat overnight to heat up the school the following morning. Storage of heat for this duration would not be cost effective.

However, if a large thermal mass is available, sharp swings in temperatures in conservatories are reduced in magnitude. Though the effectiveness of thermal mass in a conservatory is reduced due to the high conductance to the ambient environment, directly insolated surfaces are readily available, which are usually sparsely furnished, uncarpeted, and have hard, heavy-weight finishes, emphasising their periodic occupation and the transitional nature of such a space between indoors and outdoors.

The main effect of a large thermal mass in the conservatory is to elevate the minimum and reduce the peak temperatures. This can be more significant than energy saving, because the conservatory may form a glazed street or contain plants which require protection from frost and excessive temperature. A temperature elevation of 3°C above ambient is often sufficient, but low minimum temperatures might tempt the occupants to partially heat such areas, which would be undesirable. The design strategy for controlling the tendency to overheat should be the provision of adequate natural ventilation and shading, and the use of hard paving and thermal mass.

3.3 Trombe-Michel walls

Another way to provide thermal mass is to incorporate a Trombe-Michel wall.

A Trombe-Michel wall consists essentially of a glazed cavity fronting a mass absorber wall. The wall absorbs short-wave solar radiation and re-emits it as long wave thermal radiation. This is effectively trapped in the cavity and causes the temperature of the air and the wall to rise.

As a consequence of the wall's heavy thermal mass there is a considerable time delay, amounting to several hours, between the absorption of the solar radiation and transmission of the heat through the wall to the room behind.

The Trombe-Michel wall can be used to provide thermal mass. It is essentially a glazed cavity fronting a solid mass absorber wall.

The water absorber type wall engenders certain practical problems and its transparent qualities can be better provided by transparent insulation material.

Air is allowed to pass between the cavity and the room, effectively operating in a thermo-syphoning mode, with heat flow to the room occurring via convection.

The stack effect can be used to ventilate the space adjacent to the Trombe wall.

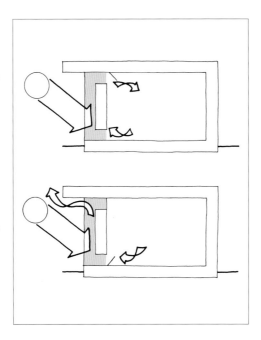

Vents may be provided at the top and bottom of the cavity to allow air to pass between the cavity and the room. Thus the time lag is reduced and the wall is effectively operating in a thermo-syphoning mode with heat flow to the room occurring via convection. The normal mode of operation is to close the vents during the day and open them when heating is required in the room.

There are very few examples of the incorporation of a Trombe-Michel wall in UK school design and some of these are not very successful. Most schools are used only during the day, therefore the availability of heat in the late afternoon and evening is not normally an advantage. For this reason the use of Trombe-Michel walls in UK schools is limited. Indeed much of the energy absorbed by such a wall is wasted, whereas the use of a normal direct gain window could provide daylight and reduce the need for electric lighting.

Looe Junior and Infants School (see case study) in Cornwall incorporates a mini-Trombe wall, topped by a concrete worktop, which was intended to moderate temperature swings and reduce heating loads by taking advantage of solar gains. But this design of Trombe wall has also not been very effective.

3.4 Thermo-syphoning air panels

There has been comparatively little commercial development of the thermo-syphoning air panel to date. The simplest thermo-syphoning air panels have the absorber plate attached to the rear panel of the collector, so that air passes between the glazing and the absorber. The disadvantage of this configuration is that air convects over the glazing and heat is lost to the exterior, and a dust and smoke film may gradually form on the inner surface of the glass. This reduces the transmittance of the cover and detracts from the appearance of the system.

The amount of dust which accumulates will depend on the cleanliness of the room air and the amount of condensation which forms on the inner surface of the glazing. These problems have led to panel designs in which air is passed behind the absorber plate, so isolating the moving air stream from the glazing. The layer of air contained between the absorber panel and the glazing provides insulation, whilst the inner surface of the cover is kept free from dust. In this 'back-pass' configuration, the airtightness of the cover is not crucial to the performance of the collector. Such units are potentially maintenance free. However the air space between the glazing and the absorber makes the collector deeper than a 'front-pass' design.

Thermo-syphoning air panels have been included as an integral part of a newly-built school and in contrast have formed part of a cladding system installed as part of a building refurbishment at Nazeing County Primary School (see case study). In this latter case, however, initial results suggest disappointingly long pay-back periods, mainly due to the high manufacturing costs attributed to prototype development for a limited-scale pilot project.

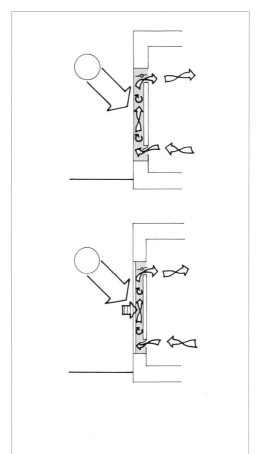

A simple front pass thermo-syphoning panel with the absorber plate attached to the rear panel of the collector, so that air passes between the glazing and the absorber.

In the back-pass thermo-syphoning panel, air is passed behind the absorber plate, isolating the moving air stream from the glazing.

3.5 Roof-space collectors

A roof-space collector is essentially a pitched roof which is used to provide warm air, and is often partially or fully glazed on its southerly aspect. In which case, the roof space is frequently painted matt black internally in order to enhance the collection of solar energy.

The roof-space collector is replenished with air either from within the dwelling or from the outside. Solar-heated air from the roof-space collector is conveyed by an automatically-controlled fan, via a duct, either directly into the classroom or as a pre-heated supply to a warm air space-heating system.

A roof-space collector involves the passive collection and active distribution of solar heat and is thus, generically, a hybrid solar energy system. Heat is stored within the structural and thermal-mass elements of the roof-space collector. Ventilation is employed to prevent overheating in high summer.

Five principal modes of operation of a roof-space collector can be identified. They are:

(i) During daytime conditions, when the temperature of the roof-space collector is above that of the building, a thermostatically-controlled fan continually takes air from the building. This air is passed through the roof-space collector, where it is warmed and returned to the building. This mode is suitable for schools, as they are occupied during the day.

(ii) Air is heated as it passes, under the action of the fan from the outside into the heated building via the roof-space collector. The volumetric flow rate through the fan in this case will be less than that used for mode (iii) operation. If this air forms a large proportion of the total ventilation then this mode provides pre-heating of the ventilation air. Unlike modes (i) and (iii), the roof-space collector does not have to be at a temperature above that of the building to

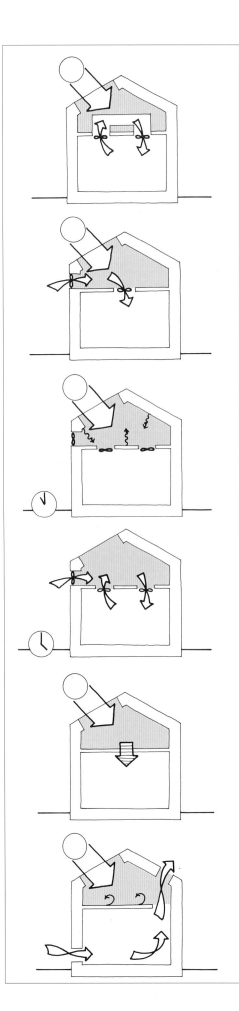

i. Air is passed through the roof-space collector, is warmed and returned to the building.

ii. Air is heated as it passes under the action of the fan from the outside into the heated building via the roof-space collector.

iiia. During the day the roof-space rises in temperature as solar energy is collected.

iiib. In the late afternoon, the stored heat is harnessed and warm air is conveyed from the roof-space collector by a fan.

iv. Heat is passed by conduction through the floor of the roof-space collector.

v. Buoyancy-driven flow occurs which draws air into the roof-space collector from the building and thence outside.

provide a beneficial effect, because any warming of the air as it passes through the attic space will provide some reduction of the ventilation load. As buildings become better insulated, so the proportion of energy used to heat ventilation air will become greater. Roof-space collectors operating in this mode are thus compatible with and complement the use of energy thrift measures in buildings.

(iii) During the day, the roof space rises in temperature as solar energy is collected and no forced circulation of air occurs through the system. In the late afternoon, the stored heat is harnessed. Warm air is conveyed from the roof-space collector by a fan. The replenished air to the attic may be supplied from either inside or outside the building. This mode is not usually appropriate for school buildings, but is useful for buildings not occupied during the day.

(iv) Heat is passed by conduction through the floor of the roof-space collector. This will frequently have little effect as the floor of a roof-space collector is well insulated. Good floor insulation is recommended, otherwise it is likely that the total diurnal losses would exceed the gains, except perhaps if the roof-space collector were double glazed and fitted with an insulating night-blind. In this mode, the roof-space collector acts as a buffer space between the ceiling of the uppermost storey and the outdoor environment, thereby reducing the heat losses from the roof of the building.

(v) Buoyancy-driven flow occurs which draws air into the roof-space collector from the building and thence outside. The replenishing flow of air into the building is from the ambient external environment. In this mode, the roof-space collector is inducing ventilative cooling as required in hot weather.

The advantage of a roof-space collector is that it can have a low initial capital cost, as its physical construction may not differ greatly from that of a conventional pitched roof. In addition, a reduction in initial cost can arise from the employment of components (i.e. fans and controls) that would be already present in a warm air heating system. A roof-space collector need not necessarily be glazed, and whether or not it is glazed, it should be most effective for buildings used during daylight hours. Relatively high roof-space collector temperatures are possible.

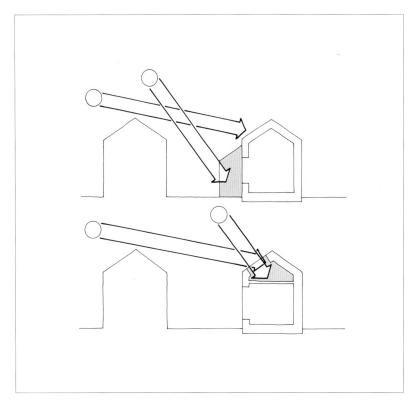

Fewer site planning constraints are required to ensure that roof-space collectors are not overshadowed. This contrasts with passive solar systems at ground floor level in high-density urban locations which may suffer levels of overshadowing at lower sun angles that make the passive solar elements ineffective.

Chapter 4 Economic and energy appraisals

It is difficult to undertake an economic appraisal of a particular passive solar feature of a building for two reasons. The first is the difficulty in isolating the cost of the building feature. The second is identifying the energy savings and maintenance costs of the feature over the life of the building of 60 to 100 years. Given the uncertainties involved in such an analysis, very few, if any, meaningful conclusions can be drawn from such an exercise. Hence this section of the bulletin simply looks at total costs of schools with passive solar features and examines their energy performances.

4.1 Cost analysis

Tender costs for 35 passive solar schools were investigated. The costs were obtained generally from published sources and local authorities. All prices are adjusted to be correct to fourth-quarter 1992 price levels.

The interquartile average cost of the 35 schools looked at is £461/m². This compares well with the national interquartile average for all schools of £476/m². [This is based on the cost of 918 new schools and major extensions built between 1986 and 1992.] Figure 4.1 shows the cost of all the passive solar schools. Also drawn on the graph are lines indicating the passive solar and national averages mentioned above. It can be clearly seen that while a few solar schools cost a great deal more, most solar schools are of similar cost to ordinary schools. The costs are generally well within 10% of those recommended by DFE for new buildings. Table 4.1 gives details of the costs and floor areas of the schools.

4.2 Energy consumption comparison

For many of the schools looked at, the energy consumption was regularly monitored so figures were readily available. To analyse the energy performance of the buildings, their calculated design Annual Energy Consumption Value in primary energy units (as defined by Design Note 17) was compared with the actual AECV which was worked out from known consumption figures. Figure 4.2 and Table 4.2 show the two sets of AECVs. Both figures were available for 12 schools. Also shown on Figure 4.2 are AECV average monitored values for the UK (excluding kitchen use) of 332kWh/m² for secondary schools and 302kWh/m² for primary schools (calculated from the figures in CIBSE Guide Volume F Table 2.16) and also the DN 17 maximum of 300kWh/m² for a typical new primary school of 1400m².

It can be seen from Table 4.2 that the calculated AECVs for all the passive solar schools are below the DN 17 maximum of 300kwh/m² and in most cases well below.

DN17 excludes kitchen and process loads (e.g. kilns and swimming pools) and use out of normal school hours. In calculating Actual AECVs these elements of the energy consumption have been excluded. DN17 also uses a steady-state estimate of energy consumption and is therefore less accurate than some of the more detailed computer simulations. Its advantages are speed and simplicity, which are useful at the early design stage.

In most situations passive solar schools would use less energy than traditional schools of equivalent size. Other independent studies have shown that passive solar schools can use 10% - 30% less than other similar schools.

Conclusion on energy use and capital cost

In conclusion it can be said that schools in the UK with passive solar features need not cost any more than ordinary schools, and if the passive solar features are carefully chosen and properly designed, then the school will be more energy efficient and should use at least 10% less energy.

Table 4.1 Passive solar schools, costs, and floor areas

School name	Type	Local Authority	Gross Floor area square metres	Capital Cost £/square metre	Date of Tender	Cost at 4Q92 per square metre corrected for location
Tendring	secondary	Essex	1,015	196.45	1Q 79	322.03
Walmley	first and middle	Birmingham	2,161	228.82	1Q79	367.28
Bosmere	middle	Hampshire	1,734	286.21	1Q 82	369.29
Hook	infants and junior	Hampshire	2,586	311.48	1Q 85	370.70
Looe	infants and junior	Cornwall	1,374	299.65	4Q 82	384.47
Cherrytree	primary	Essex	1,059	191.21	4Q 77	389.35
Aspull	primary	Wigan	912	318.12	1Q 81	393.87
Frogmore	secondary	Hampshire	1,611	242.91	1Q 79	398.19
St Peter's	primary	Essex	1,149	339.11	2Q 84	403.58
Methilhill	primary	Fife	3,168	476.6	2Q 88	409.54
Hulbert	middle	Hampshire	1,548	315.28	4Q 81	416.97
Mistley Norman	primary	Essex	726	320.89	1Q 80	418.18
Poulton Lancelyn	primary	Wirral	1,116	410.4	4Q 86	418.97
St Thomas, Leigh	primary	Wigan	661	370.18	4Q 83	425.43
Great Leighs	primary	Essex	699	305.42	1Q 80	434.48
Nabbotts	junior	Essex	880	345.06	4Q 82	442.73
Thorpe Bay	secondary	Essex	7,452	345.33	2Q 82	445.01
Ravenscroft	primary	Essex	1,001	348.04	4Q 80	449.07
Perronet Thompson	secondary	Humberside	9,947	427.57	2Q 86	454.13
Newlands	primary	Hampshire	910	207.51	2Q 77	454.49
Roach Vale	primary	Essex	1,119	201.91	1Q 77	469.87
Ushaw Moor	primary	Durham	1,150	354.83	4Q 81	479.37
Farnborough Tech.	Further Education	Hampshire	11,179	390.52	4Q 83	487.01
St. Cleer	primary	Cornwall	604	378.09	4Q 81	516.34
Ashford Godinton	primary	Kent	847	303.42	2Q 78	517.96
Holywell	primary	Nottingham	810	418.95	2Q 80	523.79
St Mary's	secondary	Wirral	2,133	60.55	1961	538.22
Leith Academy	secondary/community	Lothian	9,295	731.28	2Q 88	560.45
Fleet	Infants	Hampshire	1,188	548.62	2Q 87	562.96
Netley	Infants	Hampshire	835	444.32	1Q 83	564.16
Barnes Farm	Infants	Essex	704	537.44	2Q 86	594.86
Cabot City Tech. Col.	secondary	Avon	8,550	601.26	4Q 92	626.31
Dickleburgh V.C.	primary	Norfolk	520	528.85	1Q 84	628.51
Swanlea	secondary	L.B.Tower Hamlets	9,023	773.78	4Q 93	745.81
Green Park	primary	Bucks	1,400	862.48	2Q 90	746.14
Fencedyke	primary	Strathclyde	1,309	356.82	2Q 76	808.26

Interquartile average of passive solar schools   461.20

National interquartile average of 918 new schools and major extensions   475.79
built between 1986 and 1992

Table 4.2 Annual consumption of primary energy (in kWh per square metre of gross floor area)

	Calculated AECV	Actual AECV	Ratio of Actual AECV / Calculated AECV
St Mary's, secondary		97	
Frogmore, secondary extension	103		
St Peter's, primary	141	98	0.70
Walmley, infants	153	131	0.86
Newlands, primary	174	130	0.75
Swanlea, secondary	153		
Ravenscroft, primary	135	177	1.31
Cabot City Technology College, secondary	173		
Netley Abbey, infants		174	
Tendring, secondary	180		
Hartsfield, primary		191	
Bosmere, middle	191		
Hook, infants and junior	246	206	0.84
Great Leighs, primary	249	207	0.83
Barnes Farm, infants	296	171	0.58
Nazeing County, primary		236	
St Thomas Leigh, primary	250	230	0.92
Holywell, primary	236	262	1.11
Looe, junior and infants	242	257	1.06
Mistley Norman, primary	249	255	1.02
Dickleburgh V.C., primary		254	
Fleet, infants		256	
Roach Vale, primary	258	274	1.06
Perronet Thompson, secondary		270	
Farnborough Technology College, F.E.	275		
Cherry Tree, primary		276	
Poulton Lancelyn, primary		302	
Leith Academy, secondary		309	
Thorpe Bay, secondary		344	
Ushaw Moor, junior		405	
Aspull, primary		492	
Average values of passive solar schools	**211**	**207**	**0.92**

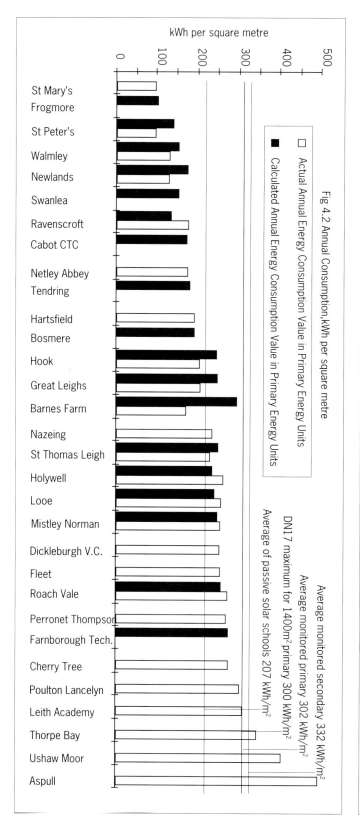

Fig 4.2 Annual Consumption,kWh per square metre

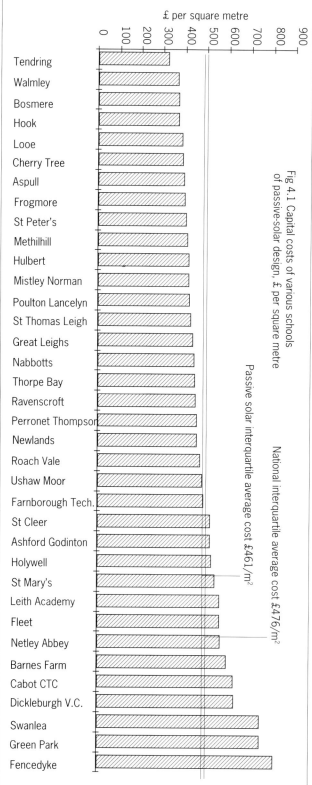

Fig 4.1 Capital costs of various schools of passive-solar design, £ per square metre

Chapter 5 Case studies

	Central atrium	Conservatory	Trombe wall	Thermo-syphoning air panel	Roof-space collector	Direct gain	External shading
Aspull Primary	○						
Barnes Farm Infants	○						
Cabot City Technology College	○	○				○	○
Cherry Tree Primary	○						
Fleet Infants						○	○
Great Leighs Primary		○					
Hook Infants' and Junior	○						○
Leith Academy Secondary	○						
Looe Junior and Infants			○				○
Nazeing Primary				○			
Netley Abbey Infants	○				○		
Newlands Junior	○						○
Perronet Thompson Comprehensive	○						
St Peter's Primary	○						
Roach Vale Primary	○						
Swanlea Secondary	○						
Thorpe Bay High	○						

Aspull Church School

Location

Bolton Road, Aspull, Wigan.

Design

In common with the 'atria' schools of Hampshire and Essex, the atrium was included in this building as a means of providing extra space within the school at low cost. However, this design differs in that the atrium is heated and is used even during midwinter.

Form

The atrium is effectively the heart of the building, providing nearly all of the circulation space for the two classroom blocks, the administration zone and the hall and kitchen areas which surround it. There is no corridor space in the school.

Construction

The site is very exposed and subject to strong winds, consequently a great deal of attention has been paid to the successful sealing of doors.

Passive features

Whilst the atrium is heated, and not an obvious passive solar exemplar, air heated in the atrium during periods of solar gain and low ambient temperature is distributed to the classrooms to provide heating. Instead of being merely gained space and a buffer against inclement weather, the atrium can make a positive contribution to the heating of the entire building: classroom doors are opened when the atrium is charged with solar heated air, so that the warm air can permeate the teaching areas.

On a cloudy summer's day, there was a noticeable difference in temperature

Plan of Aspull Church School. The atrium not only acts as a passive solar feature, but provides nearly all the circulation space for the school.

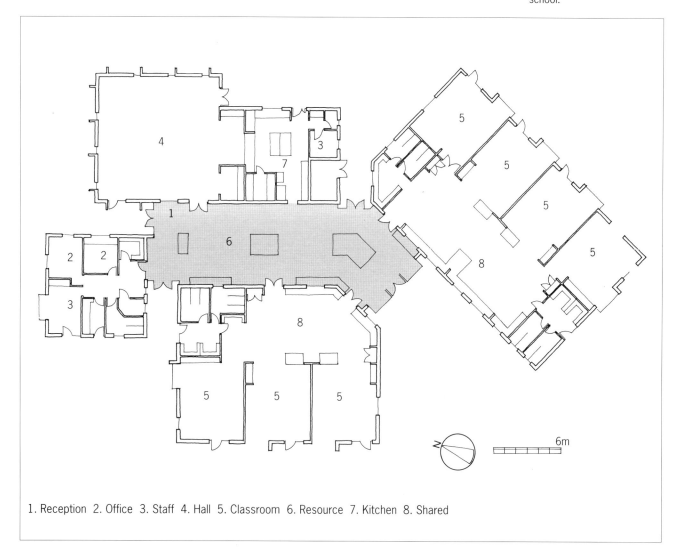

1. Reception 2. Office 3. Staff 4. Hall 5. Classroom 6. Resource 7. Kitchen 8. Shared

Section through one of the teaching blocks showing the roof configuration and rooflights.

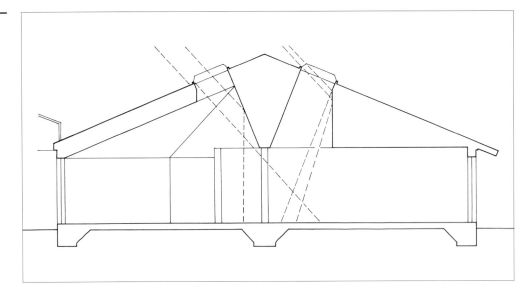

occuring between the atrium and the classbases: this no doubt encourages staff to open classroom doors in order to gain benefit from the warm air in the atrium when appropriate.

Heating and ventilation

Daytime heating in the classrooms is controlled by a sensor in the atrium plus local controls on the heating equipment. An optimiser adjusts the start time of the heating, so that the required temperature is achieved at the start of occupation and not before.

During cold weather with no solar gains, the temperature of the atrium is maintained by fan convector heaters which form part of the school's gas-fired water heating system. The roof of the atrium is twin-walled polycarbonate and ventilation louvres are provided around the edge of the structure rather than along the ridge. There are two or three days in the school year when the enclosure overheats and cannot be used between the hours of 10 a.m. and 3 p.m. (The atrium is oriented slightly west of north/south). Similarly there are two or three days when exceptionally cold north winds blow and the glazed area is too cold to use.

Lighting

During dull days, the natural lighting in the atrium is supplemented with artificial light. The level of daylighting in the classrooms was satisfactory, but artificial lighting was used to supplement this at all times.

Amenity

The naturally-lit environment in the atrium, with growing plants, is very popular; the library and craft equipment are permanent features. In contrast to other 'atria' schools, the staff of Aspull consider that such an area should be available all year round.

Energy and Building Statistics

Annual Energy Consumption:
Gas (metered)
(Heating, hot water, cooking) 211,032 kWh
Electricity 38,500 kWh
Total 249,532 kWh

Estimated catering consumption:
Gas 20517 kWh
Electricity 4000 kWh

Actual Annual Primary Energy Consumption
(corrected for location but not for 20 year Degree-Day average and excluding catering)
= 448,750 kWh or 492 kWh/m^2

Gross floor area: 912m^2 (including atrium which is heated in winter)
Teaching area: 466m^2
Number of pupil places: 210
Building Net Cost (BNC): £290,125
Base date: March 1981
BNC/gross floor area: £318.12/m^2
Completed: March 1984.

Client

Wigan Metropolitan Borough Council.

Architecture

J. Buxton, Ellis Williams Partnership.

Conclusions

The head teacher was appointed prior to the completion of the school and was involved in the fine-tuning of the building. The flexibility afforded by the semi open-plan design was appreciated; the layout of the school was such that the movement of the children via the atrium did not interfere with the teaching that went on within it. The attitude of the staff was that there is no such thing as a periodically used space in a school building. Therefore the atrium is always heated. The penalty for heating the atrium can be seen in the high energy use.

Barnes Farm Infants' School

Location

Henniker Gate, Chelmsford, CM2 6QH, Essex, 51.6N 0.41E.

There are two schools on this site; the Infants' School, which was occupied in January 1988, and the Junior School, which is a system building, similar to Cherry Tree Primary, completed in 1980.

Design

The Infants School is similar in design to the Newlands School in Hampshire, in that it features an unheated atrium/greenhouse which joins two school blocks. The atrium is oriented along a north-south axis and classrooms are incorporated in both blocks. There is no significant direct gain element to this school.

Form

The two teaching blocks of the Infants' School are joined by a long atrium, thereby providing a low cost additional area which functions both as a covered courtyard and covered external teaching space. It contains a library area and is used for technology and cooking. This 'buffer zone' has allowed the use of extensive glazing in the walls of the classrooms adjacent to it.

Construction

The external cavity walls have an external skin of 100 mm concrete blocks, a 50 mm cavity and 160 mm fair-faced Lignatherm blocks internally. The walls have aluminium single glazed vertical sliding sash windows, with a polyester powder finish.

The atrium is glazed with twin-walled polycarbonate. The roof trusses in the classroom blocks are visible and those on the gable ends are glazed to provide daylight.

The low-pitched roof is covered in cement fibre sheeting.

Plan of Barnes Farm Infants' School. In clement weather the classrooms can be opened to the atrium.

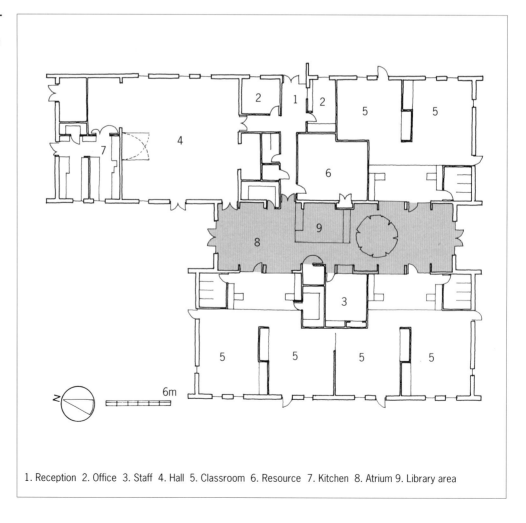

1. Reception 2. Office 3. Staff 4. Hall 5. Classroom 6. Resource 7. Kitchen 8. Atrium 9. Library area

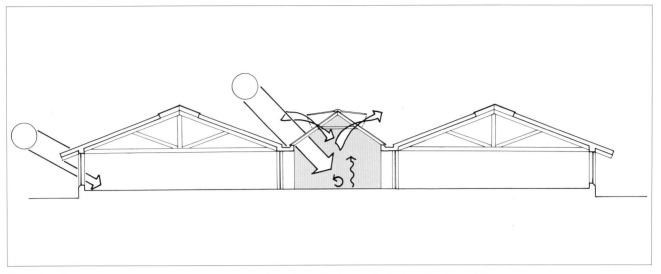

Passive features

The unheated atrium was constructed using greenhouse technology and includes motorised ridge vents for ventilation, operated by a rack-and-pinion mechanism. The vents are controlled manually although there is facility for automatic operation. Doors at each end of the enclosure are opened to promote ventilation during warm periods. There is no heating in the atrium as it was not intended to be used as teaching space year round, but as additional covered space. However its use as a library suggests it would be useful to use the space all the time. There have been attempts to heat this space by leaving classroom doors open and using warm air from these areas to heat it. The atrium may be entered from the classrooms via doors or sliding glass partitions. During clement weather, the classrooms may be opened to the atrium.

Heating and ventilation

The motorised butterfly ridge vents installed to provide summer ventilation may only be effective if sufficient low level inlet flow paths are available, i.e. the end doors may be required to be open.

Lighting

The extensive use of glass along both classroom/atrium walls ensures good daylighting of the classrooms. The classrooms also enjoy a high level of daylighting via solar-resistant double glazed rooflights and glazing in the gable ends. Artificial light is provided by uplighting of the sloping underside of the roof. There were complaints of glare from the glazing in one classroom which faced southeast.

However, the combination of uplighting and natural lighting was considered to be very restful and it was popular with staff and a welcome alternative to fluorescent lighting.

The north-south alignment of the atrium ridge facilitates the attainment of good daylighting, as the low winter sun-light is allowed in from the south facing gable-end windows, whilst in addition it inhibits overheating in summer.

Amenity

The atrium is a very popular feature of the building and there were no complaints of cold air from this space entering the class-bases.

Section through the two teaching blocks and the unheated atrium, which has been a popular feature of the school.

Energy and Building Statistics

Calculated Annual Primary Energy Consumption = 296 KWh/m²

Actual Average Annual Primary Energy Consumption of both schools combined (corrected from region and annual degree days to national 20 year DD average and to exclude catering) = 171 kWh/m²

Gross floor area: 700m²
Unheated atrium: 140m²
Number of pupil places: 180
Building Net Cost (BNC): £378,358 excluding external works
External works: £66,269
[Base date 2nd Quarter 1986]
BNC/gross floor area: £537.44/m²
Completed in 1988.

Client

Essex County Council.

Architecture

L. Wood, County Architect's Dept.,
Essex County Council.

Conclusions

This is a good example of an unheated atrium. The atrium width of 6.2 m is optimal. The vents are effective in preventing overheating. Automatic control of the vents would be preferable to prevent overheating but manual over-ride would be needed to allow for sudden changes in the weather.

The south facade showing the entrance to the central atrium

Internal view of the unheated atrium

John Cabot City Technology College

Location

Woodside Road, Kingswood, Bristol. The site falls away both to the north and to the west and the area which could be developed was severely restricted. There is a good view in the northwest direction towards the new grass amphitheatre and existing orchard, which are at the focus of the new crescent block.

Design

This is an innovative design for minimum environmental impact, using simple, easily comprehensible environmental controls including a Building Management System, and natural ventilation and daylighting of deep-plan spaces where possible. Teaching spaces are of high quality and responsive to the external climate.

Form

The crescent-shaped spine runs roughly northeast to southwest and is the primary circulation route through which the main parts of the building are approached. At the north end of the street is the administration office, entrance atrium, main hall and dining room. At the south end of the street is the sports hall, placed at the lowest level of the site. Running southeast off the street are three 2-storey, deep-plan classroom blocks. The layout of the building is intended to provide specific principle circulation routes and side streets and public spaces that provide many opportunities for social interaction. The circulation is designed to reinforce departmental identities. The design philosophy is similar to that of Leith Academy (see case study).

Construction

The building is steel framed with brick walls and aluminium framed windows and curtain walling infill and cladding. The exposed steel columns on both the wings and the crescent, provide fixings for the solar shading, structural support for the roof and act as rainwater down-pipes. The thermally broken aluminium windows are double glazed and powder coated.

The majority of the roofing is low profile metal decking but terne coated stainless steel is used on the curved part of the crescent. Floors are cast in-situ concrete slabs on reinforced strip footings under column lines. Wall finishes are either plastered or fair-faced brickwork. There is a suspended ceiling on the ground floor, to allow for service runs. The acoustic lining on the upper floor follows the roof line.

Passive features

The exposed floor mass in the street absorbs heat from the winter sun. Extensive motorised translucent solar blinds allow 65% of the external wall to be glazed to minimise energy use by using daylight, whilst preventing summer overheating. The classroom wings are designed to maximise the use of daylight and natural ventilation.

Heating and ventilation

Natural ventilation inlets and outlets have been designed for all spaces. Some of the air inlets are combined with warm air heaters and the outlets are controlled automatically.

The classroom wings have ventilation shafts down to the ground floor. These provide cross-ventilation to the deep plan. Heating is extensively zoned and controlled by a Building Energy Management System (BMS) with a central computer and printer. One of the three gas-fired boilers is condensing and supplies a low-temperature underfloor heating system in the entrance atrium, main hall, and drama space.

Warm air heating systems provide a fast response in the sports hall, sports changing room, kitchen and dining room. Classroom blocks and circulation areas have radiators.

Direct gas-fired storage water heaters are provided in the sports changing rooms and kitchen and point-of-use electric water heaters are used in toilets and teaching areas.

Cooling is only provided to the business studies room where there are a lot of computers..

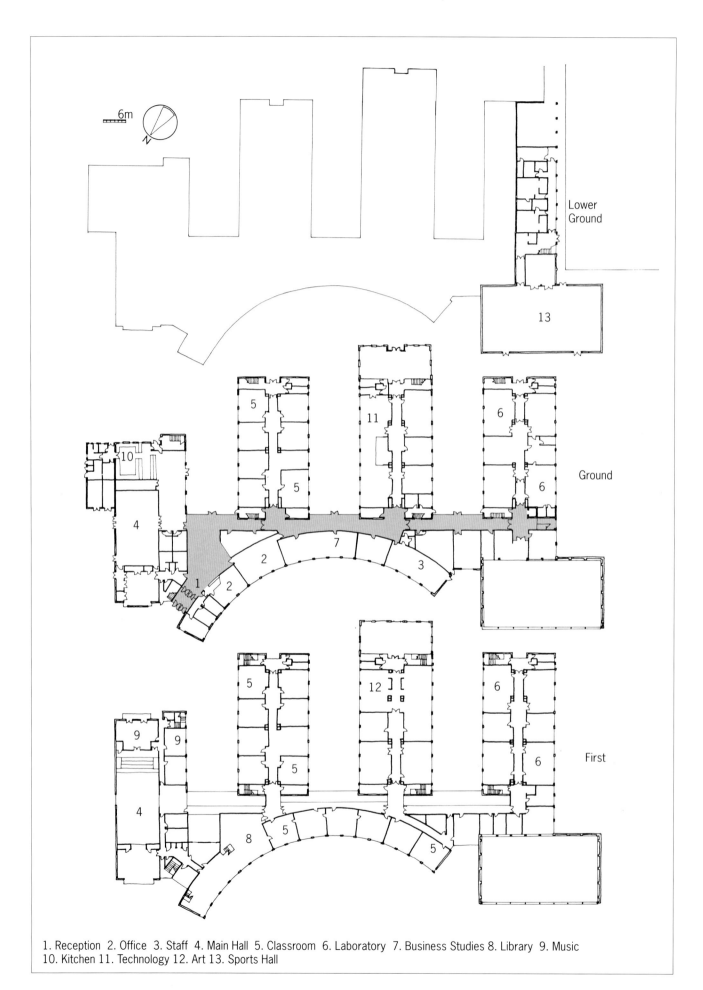

1. Reception 2. Office 3. Staff 4. Main Hall 5. Classroom 6. Laboratory 7. Business Studies 8. Library 9. Music
10. Kitchen 11. Technology 12. Art 13. Sports Hall

Side of classroom block showing fixed horizontal shading and multi-coloured motorised vertical translucent blinds [Simon Doling]

Lighting

Recessed fluorescent fittings on the ground floor and surface mounted fittings on the first floor are fitted with high-frequency control gear and louvres to provide the necessary quality of light for frequent use of visual-display terminals. There is external access as well as security lighting and floodlighting of outdoor sports areas.

First floor science laboratory showing daylighting from two sides [Feilden Clegg Design]

Case studies

Typical section through classroom block showing ventilation ducts to ground floor and daylighting of top floor

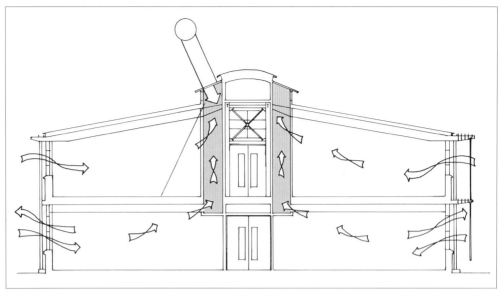

Energy

The design annual energy consumption in primary energy units is 173 kWh/m². This should be compared with the 1981 Department for Education Design Note 17 required maximum of 240 kWh/m².

Energy and Building statistics
U-values are much lower than the current Building Regulations Standards:-

	Regs.	Actual	% improvement
Walls	0.45	0.32	40%
Roofs	0.45	0.30	50%
Ground slab	0.45	0.45	

Calculated Annual Energy Consumption Value in Primary Energy Units = 173kWh/m²

Gross floor area: 8720m² excluding unheated sports store: 50m²
Teaching area: 4330m²
Number of pupil places: 900
Building Net Cost (BNC): £5,242,946 excluding external works
External works: £781,641
Base date: 4th Quarter 1992
BNC/gross floor area: £601.26/m²
Completed in 1993.

Architecture

Feilden Clegg Design.

Structural and Building Services Engineers and Quantity Surveyors

Buro Happold.

Conclusions

The constituent parts of the building are clearly visible with structure and services easily identified, e.g. the central plant room is visible from the internal street. It is a low-energy building making good use of daylight and natural ventilation and fits in with the landscape.

References

'Building which explains itself', Construction study by Tim Ostler, Architects Journal, 17 March 1993.

Model of school as viewed from the south east
[Simon Doling]

Cherry Tree Primary School
(formerly Mersea Road School)

Location

Holt Drive, Mersea Road, Colchester, C02 OBG, Essex.

Design

This 'modular component building' system-built school was the first in Essex to feature a covered courtyard with a sliding roof.

Passive features

An electrically powered sliding roof is fitted to the central courtyard and in clement weather it may be partially or totally retracted to provide ventilation.

In cold weather, heat from the classrooms and indirect gains maintain an equable temperature in this zone. The floor of the courtyard is paved and includes a drain so that (a) the floors can be cleaned after practical work, and (b) rain, which sometimes falls when the courtyard is not covered by the sliding roof, can drain away. The problem with this design is that the courtyard is exposed to the elements during ventilation. A pitched roof, with ventilation louvres, would reduce wind and rain effects. However, this courtyard feature of the school is popular with staff. It is difficult to determine how much solar heating is obtained with this design of covered courtyard. Similarly the extent to which daylight from this space contributes to the rest of the school is less obvious than with other designs such as Barnes Farm Infants.

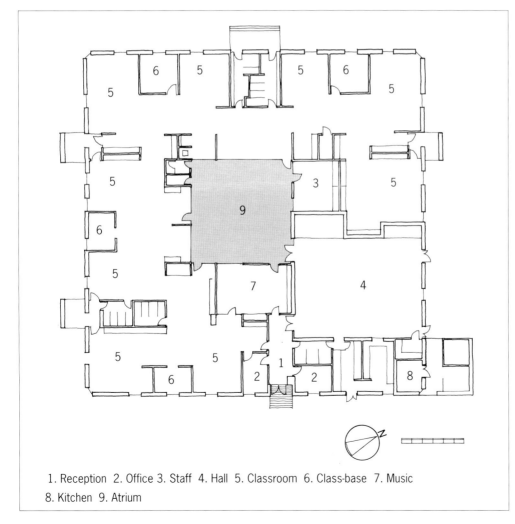

Plan of Cherry Tree Primary School. In cold weather, heat from the classrooms and indirect gains maintain an equable temperature in the central courtyard.

1. Reception 2. Office 3. Staff 4. Hall 5. Classroom 6. Class-base 7. Music
8. Kitchen 9. Atrium

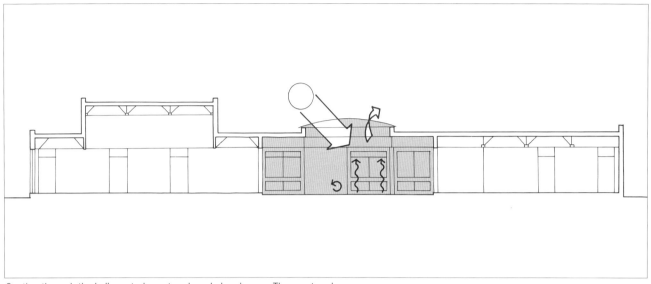

Section through the hall, central courtyard, and class-base. The courtyard has an electrically operated sliding roof which is opened in clement weather.

View from the south

Energy and Building Statistics

Annual Energy Consumption (kWh):
1986/87 electricity On Peak   27,064 kWh
                     Off Peak   4,600 kWh
        gas   172,870 kWh
1987/88 electricity On Peak   30,306 kWh
                     Off Peak   3,988 kWh
        gas   149,924 kWh
Estimated catering consumption:
        electricity On Peak   5880 kWh
        gas   37,800 kWh

Actual Average Annual Primary Energy Consumption (corrected from region and annual degree days to national 20 year DD average and to exclude catering) = 276 kWh/m²

Gross floor area: 1059m²
(excluding 92m² atrium)
Teaching area: 647m²
Unheated glazed area: 92m²

Number of pupil places: 280

Building Net Cost (BNC): £171,129 excluding external works
External works: £46,879
Base date: 4th Quarter 1977
BNC/gross floor area: £191.21/m²
Completed: 1978.

Architecture

J. F. Came, County Architect's Dept., Essex County Council.

Covered courtyard with the roof open

Fleet Infants School

Location

Velmead Road, Fleet, Hampshire. On the outskirts of the small town of Fleet in Hampshire it is sheltered by a narrow belt of pine trees to the north and looks out to the south onto more woodland across a narrow tract of sandy heathland.

Design

Nine class-bases have a southerly outlook onto paved areas. The hall/gym, music/drama room, kitchen and administration areas are on the north side of the central spine circulation route with its shared use niches. The central entrance opens onto a shared resource/library area. The administration, kitchen and toilets are in enclosed cellular pods.

Form

The building has a low-angle, pitched, profiled sheet steel roof rising to a continuous central barrel-shaped polycarbonate rooflight. It has full height double glazing on north and south facades, and a concrete slab with underfloor heating.

Construction

A minimal lightweight tubular steel frame supports a sandwich profiled steel sheet roof, containing a mineral-wool quilt, with a polythene vapour barrier and a perforated ceiling on the inside giving good acoustic absorbency.

A mesh reinforced slab is locally thickened to support the columns.

Passive features

External stretched fabric awnings on the south side protect the glazing from solar gain in summer. Ridge vents in the rooflight are opened automatically by thermostat or can be opened by a switch and are intended to generate natural ventilation for the 10 metre-deep classrooms which are fitted with perimeter louvre windows at clerestory level.

Plan of Fleet Infants School. The central spine of circulation separates the classrooms to the south from the ancillary spaces on the north side of the building.

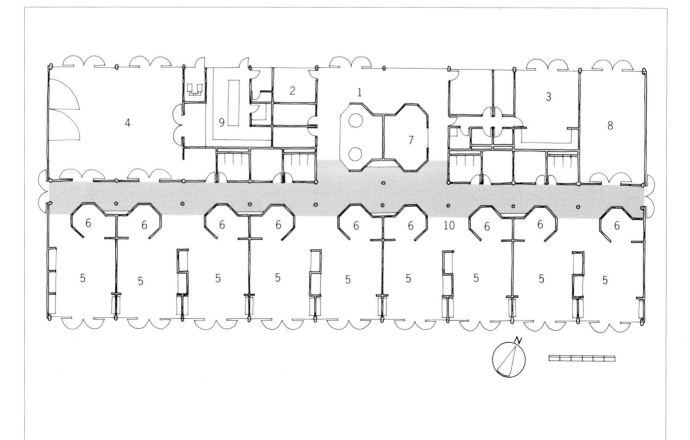

1. Reception 2. Office 3. Staff 4. Hall 5. Class-base 6. Quiet area 7. Library 8. Music 9. Kitchen 10. Shared

Heating and ventilation

The building has relatively low thermal mass in which to store solar gains and has a polythene pipe hot water underfloor heating system, which is not sufficiently responsive to accommodate such gains. Overheating has been reported during spring and autumn.

Mechanical ventilation is provided to the kitchen and toilet pods.

Lighting

Lighting is principally by daylight from the perimeter glazing and central rooflight. The quiet areas, toilets, kitchen and other areas located in pods are dependent on electric lighting.

Energy

The actual average primary energy consumption (corrected for regional differences but not to the 20 year Degree-Day average) = 256 kWh/m^2.

The energy use is high when compared with figures for other well known modern Hampshire designed schools.

The ventilation loss accounts for 41% of the energy use, as shown by the Sankey diagram. This may be due to the use of louvre-type window vents, which are notoriously leaky and were replaced in many London schools partly for this reason.

Energy and Building Statistics

Actual Annual Primary Energy Consumption (corrected for regional differences but not to the 20 year Degree-Day average and adjusted to exclude catering) = 256 kWh/m^2

Gross floor area: 1188m^2
Number of pupil places: 315
Number on roll: 220
Building Net Cost (BNC): £651,761 excluding external works
External works: £74,674
Base date: 2nd Quarter 1987
BNC/gross floor area: £548.62/m^2
Completed in December 1986.

Architects

Michael Hopkins and Partners.

Services and Structural Engineers

Buro Happold.

Sankey Diagram showing the supply and consumption of energy

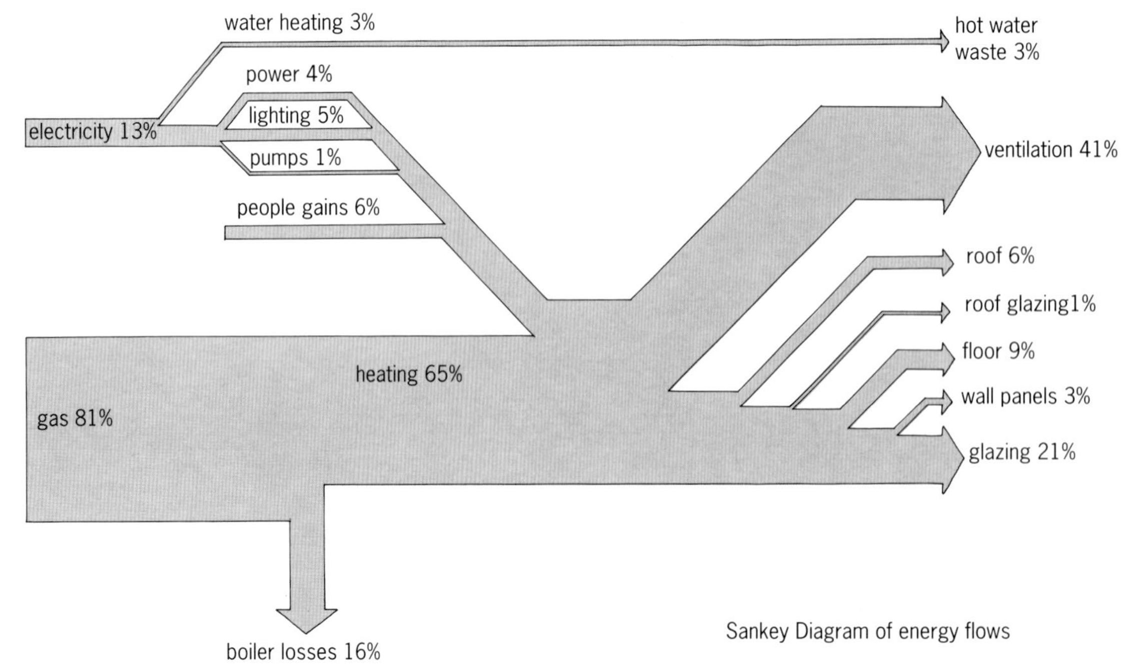

Sankey Diagram of energy flows

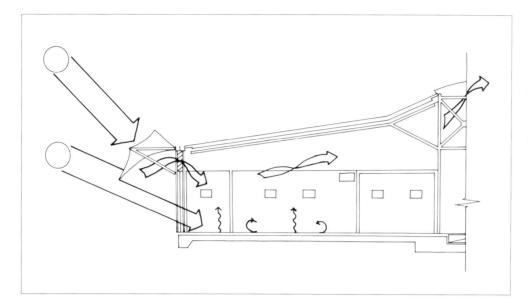

Schematic section through a classroom showing the external stretched fabric blinds which protect the glazing from summer solar gains. The ridge vents in the rooflight and the louvre windows at clerestory level help ventilate the classrooms.

Conclusions

A very popular modern design which won RIBA national and regional awards, a British Steel Construction award and a Civic Trust award. Environmental performance was considered in the design, as can be seen from the environmental section.

The rate of energy use is relatively high.

References

P. Hannay, G. Nelson & R. Barbrook, 'Setting Sail at Fleet - Velmead Infants School', Architects Journal, 30 September 1987, pp37-53.

'Patterns', Buro Happold magazine, Michael Dickson and Tony McLaughlin.

'Schools of Thought, Hampshire Architecture 1974 - 1991', Richard Weston, published by Hampshire County Council, ISBN 1 873595 10 7.

View from the east

Interior of class-base

Great Leighs Primary School

Location

Aragon Road, Great Leighs, Chelmsford, Essex, CM3 1RP.

Design

This school is one of three almost identical MCB modular system-built designs by Essex County Council (cf. Braintree Whitecourt Primary School and Mistley Norman Church of England Primary School) .

Form

The school has a square plan with five teaching bases on three sides of a full height central hall. On the fourth side is a music/drama/library room with a quiet area on the outside wall; also a kitchen and an administration area.

The hall is naturally lit, mechanically ventilated and has no immediate outside access. It provides the only circulation in the school besides the entrance corridor. The geometry of the hall roof is such that this glazing cannot be blacked-out, which is a disadvantage.

The teaching bases of the schools are arranged around the hall. They are essentially of the same design, are paired and share common practical areas which open onto the conservatories. These are effectively gained space and are partly recessed into, and partly built out from, the building.

Plan of Great Leighs Primary School

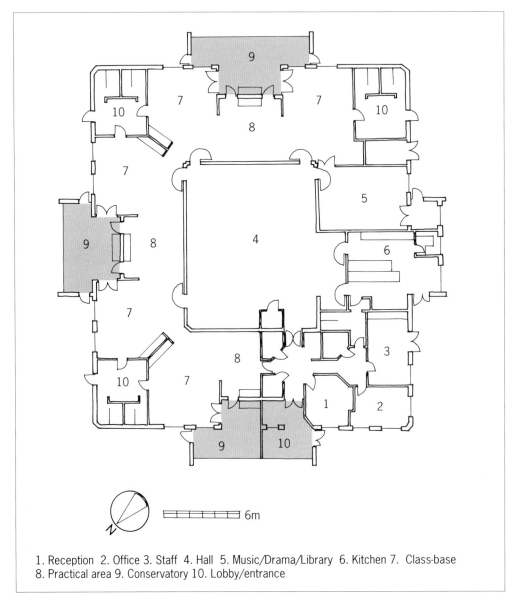

1. Reception 2. Office 3. Staff 4. Hall 5. Music/Drama/Library 6. Kitchen 7. Class-base 8. Practical area 9. Conservatory 10. Lobby/entrance

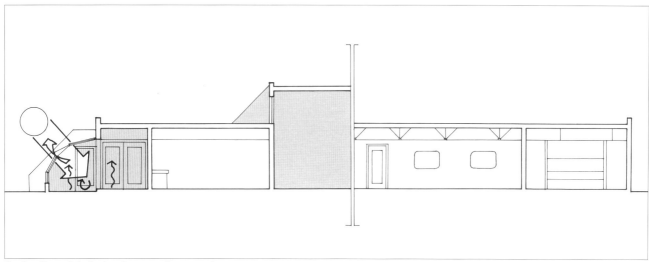

Section through hall, class-bases and conservatory

Construction

Asphalt roof, MCB steel frame, flint finish concrete wall panels, with 100 mm blockwork internally. Anodised aluminium horizontal pivot windows.

U-values:

wall	1.28 W/m²°C
roof	0.50 W/m²°C
glass	5.60 W/m²°C
floor	0.30 W/m²°C

15% of the wall area is glazed.

Passive features

An unheated conservatory is located in the middle of each of three facades. Single panel doors each side open onto external paved work areas.

Flanking walls of the conservatories are blockwork, faced internally and externally with T&G boarding. Floors have 600 square, black concrete paving slabs.

The fourth facade has the same structure, housing the kitchen entrance and music room quiet area, but here it is not fully glazed.

The conservatories of these schools originally were to have been glazed with glass, but this was too heavy for the frames, and safety perspex was substituted.

Although the designs of Great Leighs and Whitecourt schools were almost identical, they differed in two important respects; the hall of Whitecourt School had been lengthened and its roof raised to accommodate badminton playing after school hours, and a significant number of

View from the west

Conservatory and class-base

school meals were cooked in the kitchen adjacent to the hall. Consequently, the hall was reported to be unbearably hot in the summer due to a combination of heat from the kitchen and solar gains. The ventilation fans provided were considered to be both inadequate and noisy. Solar gains have been reduced by filling the twin-walled polycarbonate roof glazing with expanded polystyrene beads.

In mild weather, the conservatories at Great Leighs provide a useful area for practical activities. The same spaces at Whitecourt are used as teaching areas in an overcrowded school, in all weathers.

The orientation of the two schools is different and the Whitecourt site is more exposed.

At Whitecourt the conservatories face due north, south, east and west. The south facing conservatories are too hot at times in summer. At Great Leighs they face northeast, southeast and southwest. This produces more uniform and equable conditions through the day. The perspex at Great Leighs has discoloured and is almost opaque in the two south facing conservatories, suggesting heat as the cause. However, for some reason this has not happened at Whitecourt. Internal blinds have been installed at Great Leighs. Both these factors mean that the solar gain at Great Leighs is less.

A complaint levelled against the conservatories at the Whitecourt School, but not at Great Leighs, is that they inhibit ventilation of the adjacent classrooms in hot weather. Opening the doors to the conservatories results in warm air passing into the classrooms rather than out. Ventilation is therefore severely limited in the summer as classroom windows cannot be opened fully. This is a common problem with south facing conservatories. An unpleasant ingress of warm air is also experienced in classrooms adjacent to the conservatories of the Ravenscroft School in the summer.

Heating and ventilation

The conservatories are unheated and cannot therefore be used for activities throughout the winter and the south facing conservatories are too hot at times in summer.

Extract fans have been installed to and from the classrooms so that air can be moved from the conservatories into the classrooms and vice-versa, as required. However, in none of these schools were the staff familiar with the operation of the fans and in the Whitecourt School they were reported to be unused. If such features are to be installed in schools as part of a passive solar component, clear instructions for their use should be provided.

The main hall, kitchen and toilets have mechanical ventilation.

Heating is by oil-fired boilers.

Lighting

Lighting is mostly fluorescent with some tungsten. Lights are provided in the conservatories.

Internal roller blinds are fitted to the southwest and southeast conservatories. These shade the top two out of the three horizontal frames of glazing. They are only usually adjusted in summer.

Energy and Building Statistics

Calculated Annual Energy Consumption Value in Primary Energy Units: 249.3 kWh/m²

Actual Annual Energy Consumption:
86/87 Electricity 18454kWh, Oil 6568 litres
87/88 Electricity 20727kWh, Oil 6500 litres

Estimated catering consumption:
Electricity   8100 kWh

Actual Average Primary Energy Consumption Value (corrected from region and annual degree days to national 20 year DD average and to exclude catering) = 207kWh/m²
Gross floor area: 733m²
Teaching area: 420m²
Unheated atrium area: 90m²
Number of pupil places: 150

Building Net Cost (BNC): £223,870
External Works: £54,652
BNC/gross floor area: £305.42/m²
Base date: 1st Quarter 1980
Completed: 1981.

Amenity

The conservatories lead off the wet areas of the classrooms and are used for teaching, storage and a wide range of practical activities, from sand, water and role-play to ceramics, technology and art.

The conservatories provide a different kind of space from the classrooms.

A double sink with a cold water tap and a single socket outlet are provided in each conservatory. The largest conservatory for older pupils has a kiln and an air brush. The older pupils use the space for craft activities and as a retreat from the small and cramped classrooms.

The access via the classrooms to the conservatories and on to the outside is not direct enough, particularly in summer when large drawings are done outside and it is difficult to supervise work there. The barrier formed by the wall between the double sinks in the practical area of the classroom and the conservatory is a problem as it prevents easy access between the two spaces. The double doors to the classrooms can however be opened, providing freer access. An improvement to the conservatories would have been to fit kitchen type units around the entire perimeter providing working surfaces, and to provide space for a sink and a window sill facility for plants. This would have also allowed the dwarf wall to be increased in height to window sill level and the wall between the practical area and the conservatory to be opened up.

Architects, Building Services and Structural Engineers

County Architects' Department, Essex County Council.

Conclusions

Significantly, the occupants of Great Leighs School were much more favourably disposed towards their building than those of Whitecourt School. This may be attributed, in part, to the higher number of pupils in the Whitecourt School, which has four temporary classrooms. The Whitecourt staff place greater demands on the conservatories as extra teaching space rather than for craft activities as at Great Leighs. Nevertheless, it would appear from an initial comparison of the two schools, that orientation and location have had a considerable influence on the performance of the respective buildings and, in particular, the conservatories. At Great Leighs they were considered to be acceptable gained space, whereas summer overheating and extreme cold in winter were experienced in the Whitecourt conservatories. Consequently, they could not be used as extra teaching space as often as the staff of the latter building would have wished and were considered to be wasted, rather than gained space.

Overall the conservatories provide useful additional space as well as providing storage and a thermal buffer zone.

Hook Infants' and Junior School

Location

Hook, Hampshire 51.2N 5W.

Design

The project was a prototype in its approach to the maintenance and refurbishment of SCOLA system buildings and represents the first combined approach to building and site rationalisation by the County Architect with the aim of:

(a) Integration of two schools under one pitched roof, to provide shared use of facilities on a reduced site area.

(b) Upgrading of an existing building to current teaching standards within the brief for a new school.

(c) Providing an energy efficient environment to contemporary standards for both new and existing structures.

The school has been extensively increased in size and remodelled. The existing building was enlarged by extending each leg of the H-plan and adding a central glazed pitched roof which runs the length of the building, thereby creating atria between the classrooms in each leg of the H-plan.

A staff room is located at first floor level under the atrium roof.

Form

The axis of the glazed portion of the school lies in a northwest-southeast direction, the infants' school occupying the northwest and the juniors the southeast. The occupants of the north end of the building consider that the atrium is often very cold in winter.

Plan of Hook Infants and Junior School

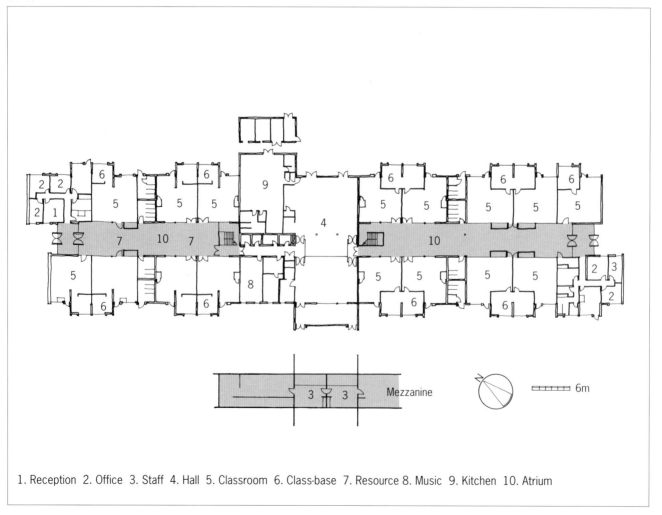

1. Reception 2. Office 3. Staff 4. Hall 5. Classroom 6. Class-base 7. Resource 8. Music 9. Kitchen 10. Atrium

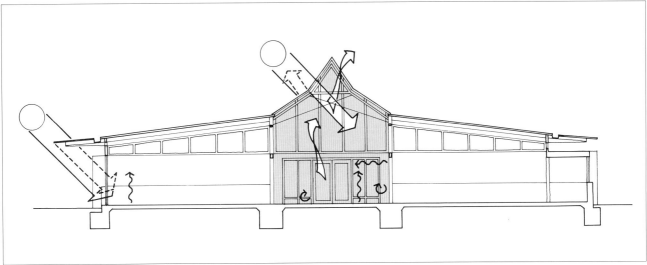

Passive features

The atria are heated. The glazed roof may also act as a source of ventilation when both high solar gains generate sufficient buoyancy and the vents are opened. The latter require manual operation. Stale air is drawn from the classroom spaces and exhausted via the roof vents. Overheating of the central glazed area during periods of high solar gain was intended to be controlled by these vents. However the size, number and mechanism for opening of these vents, are inadequate. The atrium has little thermal mass as it is carpeted. Glare is reduced by an opaque composite roof sheet attached to part of the south facing section of the pitched, glazed roof, but still causes some complaints.

Heating and ventilation

The school is primarily heated by a gas-fired central heating system, and no provision has been made for the warm air generated under the glazed roof to be conveyed for heating of the adjacent classrooms.

Lighting

Daylighting from the central areas is intended to illuminate the adjacent classrooms. Between the atria and the new classrooms there is clerestory glazing giving better daylighting than in the existing classrooms. The level of daylighting provided in the original classrooms, in contrast to the atria areas, is not considered to be satisfactory by the occupants, and artificial lighting is used at all times.

Energy

The school has been well insulated and incorporates energy-saving features, such as automatic lighting controls, which switch off the electric lighting every twenty minutes. However these lighting controls are considered by some teachers to be a nuisance at times.

Amenity

The atria are heated and carpeted, and they are used extensively as basic teaching space, as well as providing a circulation zone between the classrooms. The staff room at atrium level is sometimes unusable due to overheating.

Energy and Building Statistics

Calculated Annual Primary Energy Consumption: 246.3 kWh/m^2

Actual Annual Primary Energy Consumption: 206 kWh/m^2 (corrected from region and annual degree days to national 20 year DD average and to exclude catering)

Gross floor area of extension: 827m^2
Gross floor area of whole school: 2586m^2
Teaching area of extension: 606m^2
Teaching area of whole school: 1433m^2
Number of pupil places: 430 (original school 320)

Building Net Cost (BNC): £805,500 including external works
Base date: 1st Quarter 1985
BNC/gross floor area of whole school: £311.48/m^2
Remodelling & refurbishment completed by 1988.

Case studies

North facade

Conclusion

The atrium is popular. It is heated and used throughout the year. However it has little thermal mass as it has carpet on the floor. The ridge vents are too small and their opening mechanism is inadequate. The atrium therefore has a tendency to overheat.

Architecture

M. Ogden, Perkins Ogden Partnership, Winchester.

Building Services Engineering

G. Herman, King Cathery Partnership.

Energy Consultant

Prof. P. O'Sullivan, UWIST, Cardiff.

Interior of heated atrium. The opaque surface of the south facing roof prevents excessive solar gain, However the floor carpet reduces the thermal mass.

Leith Academy Secondary School

Location

Leith, Edinburgh.

Design

The design is planned for the management of change, with maximum flexibility and versatility and resembles a shopping centre, with a glazed main street, extensive planting, seats, a street cafe, and displays and banners identifying the subjects on offer. There are extensive community facilities and a swimming pool used by both school and community.

The secondary streets, also glazed, are orthogonal to the main street and so give access to any department without having to go through another one. The blocks of accommodation between the streets have a clear span of 16.8 metres, giving two bays of 7.2 metres each side of a 2.4 metre circulation/services distribution zone, also glazed. Sometimes this zone is incorporated within a room and sometimes it is a 'corridor' but is nevertheless wide and well lit.

Plan of Leith Academy. The glazed main and secondary streets provide independent access to all departments.

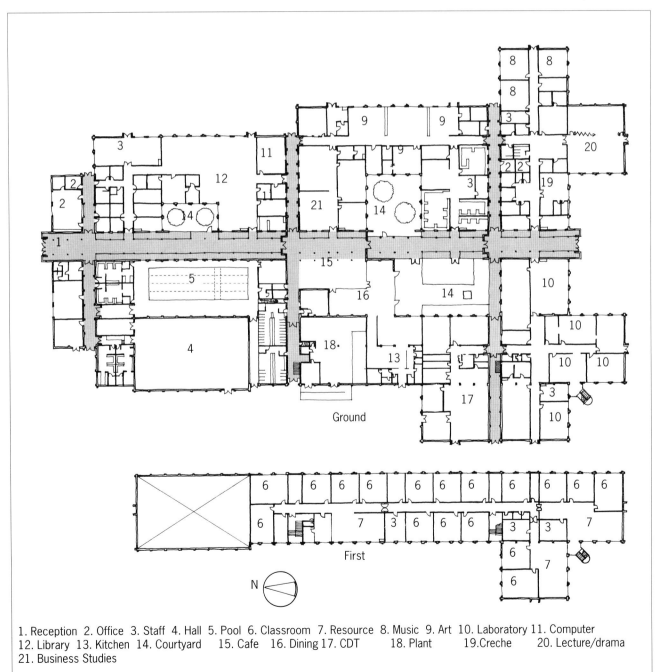

Ground

First

N

1. Reception 2. Office 3. Staff 4. Hall 5. Pool 6. Classroom 7. Resource 8. Music 9. Art 10. Laboratory 11. Computer
12. Library 13. Kitchen 14. Courtyard   15. Cafe 16. Dining 17. CDT   18. Plant   19.Creche   20. Lecture/drama
21. Business Studies

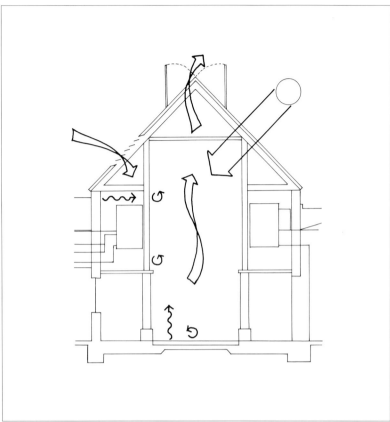

Schematic section of a street showing the glazing at roof level, with ridge vents, which help control overheating and with manual override offers assistance to the fire brigade in the event of a fire

The flexibility of the main accomodation blocks allows expansion or contraction in student numbers or changes of use. Whole blocks of the building can be sub-leased for non-educational use without affecting the rest of the school. Reorganisation is easier because all interior walls can be removed without affecting the structure or primary services.

Form

The school is predominantly single storey. On the west of the site are industrial premises and the 2 storey elements and major spaces such as the games hall are located on this side. To accommodate the poor ground conditions on the east of the site, and to fit in with the street scene of the neighbouring single storey and semi-detached private dwellings, the college is single storey along this eastern perimeter.

Construction

The structure is a steel portal frame at 3.6 m centres, spanning the full width of the 16.8 m typical building section, thus achieving the maximum unobstructed

volume. The roof is of composite insulated-steel panelling having a glazed barrel-vaulted spine at the apex above the 2.4 metre-wide circulation zone, and thereby enabling all rooms to be daylit. External walls are cavity insulated facing brick/block construction, and internal partitions are of dense paint grade concrete block. The main and secondary streets have facing blockwork insulated cavity walls, roofed with patent glazing which incorporates automatically opening sky-vents. Automatic opening louvres in secondary street doors allow the stack effect to operate to cool the streets. There are substantial areas of planting in the streets. Windows have hardwood frames and are double glazed. All glass is laminated to reduce maintenance costs. Intumescent foam in the main street glazing provides a fire barrier.

Services are generally exposed.

Passive features

The streets are glazed at roof level and so substantial solar gain occurs. The exposed solid dense concrete blocks dampen the response of the fabric to thermal swings.

To minimise overheating in summer, a series of additional ridge vents have been included in the streets. These are thermostatically controlled, and also enable smoke ventilation to be achieved at no additional cost, although smoke ventilation was not a requirement.

Dynamic energy simulation of the building was part of the in-house design process.

Heating and ventilation

Sill-line natural convection units are supplemented by warm air ducted from the air-handling units located at high level in the main north-south street.

The ductwork runs down the centre of the deep plan blocks beneath the barrel-shaped rooflights.

The streets are predominantly unheated, except for partial underfloor heating, via the residual heat from the overnight kindling of the coal-fired boilers.

The heating and ventilating is controlled by a central BMS system linked to the Council's Department of Property Services. Fresh air supply rates can be reduced in the heating season. Fresh air can be used for free cooling in summer using the supply air fans. Air-conditioning is not needed except for zones with high casual gains, e.g. due to computing equipment where local split system units have been introduced.

Lighting

By the use of clerestory glazing on corridor walls, in conjunction with slatted ceilings in smaller rooms, every room in the building is able to enjoy natural light within the deep plan.

Energy

The swimming pool has a combined heat and power plant and a heat recovery system. The NPI (National Performance Indicator, Energy Efficiency Office Yardstick) for the school is 269.8 kWh/m^2/annum which is in the Good category for a secondary school with a swimming pool and community facilities, for which the NPI ratings for Good, Average and Poor are respectively < 280, 280 to < 370, and 370 to < 470 kWh/m^2/annum.

Architect

Laura Stevenson, Property Services, Lothian Regional Council.

Conclusions

The emphasis on the changing role of the building is a concern of many designers and this building demonstrates a way of providing for a range of end uses within a single building envelope.

The design has received much attention, seems to work well and may be used as a model for further schemes including mixed-use redevelopment.

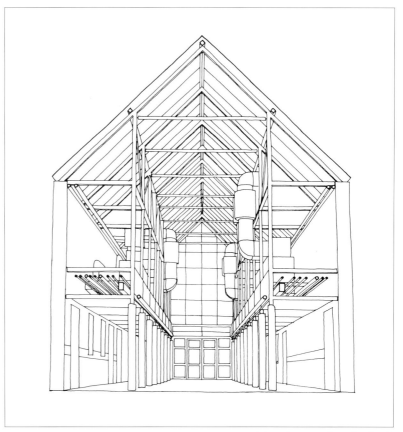

Internal perspective of a street showing the exposed ductwork and glazed roof above

Energy and Building Statistics

Actual Annual Energy Consumption
for March 1991/February 1992:
Natural gas   660,903 kWh
Coal   1,550,400 kWh
Electricity   620,652 kWh
Total   2,831,955 kWh

Estimated catering consumption:
Gas   198,000 kWh
Electricity   31,500 kWh

Conversion to Primary Energy Units (corrected from region and annual degree days to national 20 year DD average):
Natural gas   519,800 kWh
Coal   1,244,971 kWh
Electricity   1,273,268 kWh
Total   3,038,039 kWh

Actual Annual Primary Energy Consumption =309kWh/m^2 (corrected for normal secondary school hours of use without a swimming pool and to exclude catering)

Gross floor areas:
School use   7174m^2
Community use   1311m^2
Circulation space for both uses   810m^2
Total gross floor area   9295m^2
Area of unheated glazed streets 1568m^2

Number of pupil places: 900 -1500 on occasions
Building Net Cost (BNC): £6,797,293 excluding external works and preliminary ground improvements
Preliminary ground improvements: £620,832
External works: £549,815
Base date: 2nd Quarter 1988
BNC/gross floor area: £731.28/m^2
Completed in 1991.

Case studies

North facade and main
entrance from the roadway

Internal glazed street

Looe Junior and Infants' School

Location

Looe, Cornwall. On a hilltop 80 m above sea level, overlooking the town of Looe and the sea to the south and exposed to strong southwesterly winds. The site slopes gently from north to south, with a steep slope to the west.

Design

The school exploits direct gain in all of the classrooms by arranging them in an innovative cruciform plan; this avoids substantial overshading of the north wings by those to the south. An extension to the southeast wing, completed in 1988, continues the form of the original with one exception; the tiled workbenches are omitted from the Trombe-Michel walls.

Form

Shared workspaces, toilets and room for cloaks are situated on the north of the classroom wings. First floor staffroom and tankroom/bulkstore are located to the south of the hall. The entrance to the building is on the south, between the wings.

Plan of Looe Junior School. The cruciform arrangement helps avoid substantial overshading of those class-rooms on the north wings of the school.

N

6m

First Floor

1. Reception 2. Office 3. Staff 4. Hall 5. Classroom 6. Class-base 7. Library 8. Kitchen

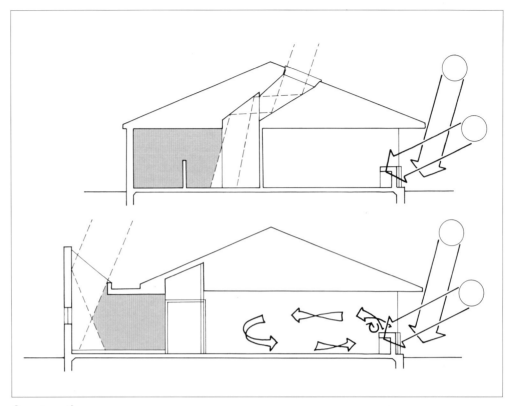

Construction

A low brick and tile building. The south facing walls of the classrooms have full height aluminium-framed double glazed windows, with the bottom 40% backed by short blockwork walls topped by tiled worksurfaces, so forming a 'Trombe bench'.

The wall construction is brick/cavity/insulation/medium-weight concrete block with 30 mm urethane foam foil-faced insulation board. Walls are built on strip foundations, with reinforced concrete ground beams and oversite slab. Partitions are thermally heavyweight. The floor contributes little to the useful thermal mass because it is carpeted. There is perimeter insulation for 1 metre around the slab.

The roof has concrete tiles with Velux rooflights and small areas of patent glazing.

Passive features

The effects of temperature variations arising from direct gains are ameliorated by the high thermal mass, and the building is well insulated. Overhanging 0.75 metre-deep eaves on the south act as fixed shading, whilst utility areas and corridors are located on the north of the building.

The 'Trombe bench', which was invented at Looe, was expected to act as a small Trombe wall. The design was untested and has not proved very effective. It has been assessed to contribute, at its peak, less than 1°C rise to room temperature, corresponding to an output of up to 2kWh, when the solar gain through the remaining glazing can be 20kWh. Even so, the idea could be worth pursuing in a modified form.

Most windows, including all rooflights, are double glazed.

There are internal sun-blinds on the classroom windows.

The internal blinds and horizontal sliding windows are difficult to use, except on still days, and there is a shortage of cross-ventilation paths. The sun shining directly through windows was cited by staff as a cause of overheating, so suggesting that glare may also be a problem.

Heating and ventilation

The hot water convectors are thermostatically controlled.

With the windows closed, because the building is very tightly constructed, the air change rate is only 0.24 air changes per hour. With the large horizontally-sliding windows open, the air change rate rises dramatically to over 10 air changes an hour (except on still days) and papers and displays are blown about. The windows do not provide adequately-controllable ventilation. However, the average ventilation rate of 2.4ac/h is roughly in line with design standards, so that the ventilation component of the heat loss will not significantly affect the overall energy performance. There are draught lobbies on all entrances.

Lighting

Although rooflights are provided to classrooms, monitoring suggests that the lights are often on when the solar intensity is low. The building makes little use of the daylight aspect of solar design, but lighting represents a minor part of the total energy use. Overhanging eaves provide fixed shading, but reduce the amount of daylight. The levels of daylight have given rise to some disappointment, with daylight factors of less than 2% in most of the classrooms.

Energy

Energy is predominantly used for space heating. The monitoring showed that the solar gains are converted into useful heating and the required controls are simple.

It was estimated by the Welsh School of Architecture, and the Building Services Consultants Databuild that some 40% of the measured average space-heating requirement is provided by solar gains.

Conclusions

This is an example of a direct gain passive solar building, which is successful in energy terms and very popular with its users. Improved future designs would make more use of daylight with better shading and more control over natural ventilation. The 'Trombe benches' were not a success.

Energy and Building Statistics
Calculated Annual Primary Energy Consumption
= 242kWh/m²

Delivered fuel use (exc. kitchen and outbuildings):
Gas   211405kWh
Electricity   16112kWh
Total   227517kWh
Actual primary energy =   352,651kWh

Actual Annual Primary Energy Consumption
= 256.7 kWh/m² (corrected from region and annual degree days to national 20 year DD average)

Gross floor area: 1374m²
Teaching area: 834m²
Number of pupil places: 300 (10 classes)

Building Net Cost (BNC): £411,725 (net cost excluding external works)
External Works: £109,173
BCIS Building Cost/GFA: £299.65/m²
Base date: 4th Quarter 1982
Completed in 1984 (extension completed in 1988).

Architecture

P. Wingrave-Newall (original building), S. Tate (extension). Cornwall County Architects Dept.

Building Services Engineering

Andrews Weatherfoil Ltd.

Structural Engineering

Jenkins and Potter.

Consultants for passive solar design

The design built on the architect's experience with St. Cleer School. Advice on the design of the extension was obtained from the Energy Studies Unit, University of Exeter.

Energy monitoring and assessment

Welsh School of Architecture and Databuild Consultants.

References

'EPA Technical Report, Looe School', December 1990, Prepared by UWIST for the Energy Technology Support Unit, Harwell, Oxfordshire.

A. Williams, 1986, 'Looe School', Building, 19, 250, 9 May, 43-50, 1986.

Anon., 'School Building in Cornwall', Brick Bulletin, 4/845, 10-11, 1985.

'Passive solar design, Looe Primary School', Architects Journal, 13 December 1989.

'Energy performance assessment of Looe Junior and Infant School' by D. K. Alexander, N. D. Vaughan, H. G. Jenkins, P. E. O'Sullivan, Ambient Energy, January 1990.

South facade showing main
entrance

South facade showing
mini-Trombe walls

Nazeing County Primary School

Location

Hyde Mead, Nazeing, Waltham Abbey, EN9 2HS, Essex. On the north side, there are low-level single storey dwellings. On the east/west sides, there is a playground and trees. On the south side, there is a playing field and no other obstructions.

Design

Thermo-syphoning air panels and double glazing were installed as part of the refurbishment of the existing school.

Construction

101 m² of thermo-syphoning air heating collectors have been incorporated in cladding panels used in the refurbishment of the single storey curtain walling. This method of retrofitting passive solar collectors enables such components to be incorporated in the fabric of existing buildings with minimal overcosts.

Passive features

The collector panels serve not only to supply heat or ventilation during periods of solar gain but also provide insulation when not in use. They can therefore be used to reduce excessive heat loss and excessive solar gains in overglazed buildings.

Such solar walls are particularly appropriate for institutional buildings which are only occupied significantly during the day, as they deliver the collected solar heat into the room with minimal time lag. Reverse circulation is prevented by locating a tedlar film damper at the collector's inlet. A manually operated actuator is used to ventilate the absorber plate in the summer to avoid overheating.

Plan of Nazeing County Primary School, showing the original curtain walling before the installation of thermo-syphoning panels

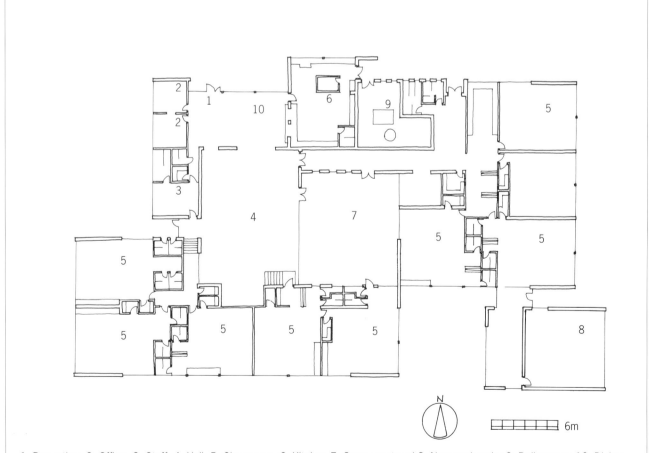

1. Reception 2. Office 3. Staff 4. Hall 5. Classroom 6. Kitchen 7. Open courtyard 8. Nursery/creche 9. Boiler room 10. Dining

Case studies

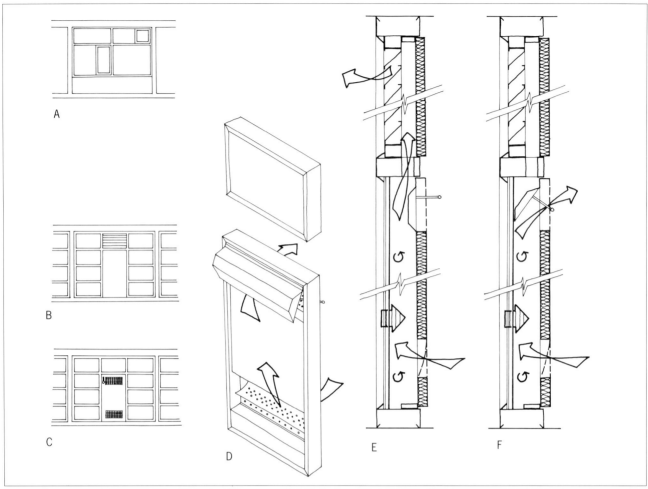

A. Original curtain wall panel.

B. Replacement thermo-syphoning panel.

C. Internal view of thermo-syphoning panel showing vents.

D. View of general arrangement of the panels.

E. Schematic showing summer operation of thermo-syphoning panel.

F. Schematic showing winter operation of thermo-syphoning panel.

Energy and Building Statistics

Actual Annual Primary Energy Consumption = 236 kWh/m² (corrected from region and annual degree days to national 20 year DD average and to exclude catering).
Gross floor area: 1632m²
Number of pupil places: 187
Cost of 36 panels of 25 different sizes: £5,888 in 1987/88
Estimated cost if part of a programme with limited number of panel sizes: £3,664 at same price base date.
Refurbishment completed in 1988.

Client

Essex County Council.

Architecture

R. Harrison, Essex County Council, Property Services Dept.

Environmental Engineering

C. Deal, Essex County Council.

Consultants for passive solar design

Collaborative Project between Essex CC, Waterloo-Ozonair, Parkside GRP; B. Norton, S. N. G. Lo, R. A. Hobday, Cranfield University.

Conclusions

The benefits of heating and ventilating derived from panels of this type should be gained at a comparable cost to that incurred where conventional curtain-wall cladding is installed.

The panels are an effective means of reducing the amount of glazing in an overglazed school and also upgrading the thermal insulation and ventilation performance. The high price and long payback period could be reduced by standardisation of panel sizes and larger production runs.

References

Norton, B., Lo, S. N. G., Hobday, R. A., (1989) 'The Development of a Passive Solar Air-Heating Collector for the Recladding of Buildings', Proc. Applied Energy Research, Inst. of Energy Conference, Swansea U.K. pp 123-133, 5-7 September.

Norton, B. & Lo, S. N. G., 1988. 'Nazeing School Thermosyphoning Air Panels', Interim report to DG XVII of the Commission of the European Communities, Brussels, Belgium, 1988.

Curtain walling before refurbishment [Essex County Council Property Services Department]

Refurbished curtain walling with thermo-syphoning air panels fitted and window area reduced [Essex County Council Property Services Department]

Interior, showing rear of thermo-syphoning panel [Essex County Council Property Services Department]

Netley Abbey Infants'

Location

Westwood Road, Netley, Hampshire. Located within an area of low-density housing.

Design

The school incorporates two elements of interest; an atrium off the main entrance and a conservatory which runs the length of the southeast facade of the building.

The conservatory is used as the main circulation space in the school, linking the teaching, music and resource areas, and is the normal entrance for the pupils.

The main entrance of the school leads into the atrium, which is well toplit and which also provides borrowed daylight for the hall. The atrium links the administration areas within the school and is used by the children as an extension to the adjoining resource area. It is not used to provide passive heating or cooling within the building. Roller blinds have been installed to reduce glare and there are seasonally adjusted vents.

Form

The main axis of the plan is southwest to northeast. The conservatory follows this direction and provides the main circulation route with seven classrooms, the hall, administration, atrium and kitchen to the north and a further two classrooms and a music room on the south side forming two garden areas.

Construction

The school has a timber frame superstructure, supported on calcium-silicate brick diaphragm walls, internally finished with pinboard or painted emulsion.

Plan of Netley Abbey Infants' School. The conservatory runs the length of the southeast facade. The atrium, which links the administration areas, can be used as an extension to the resource area.

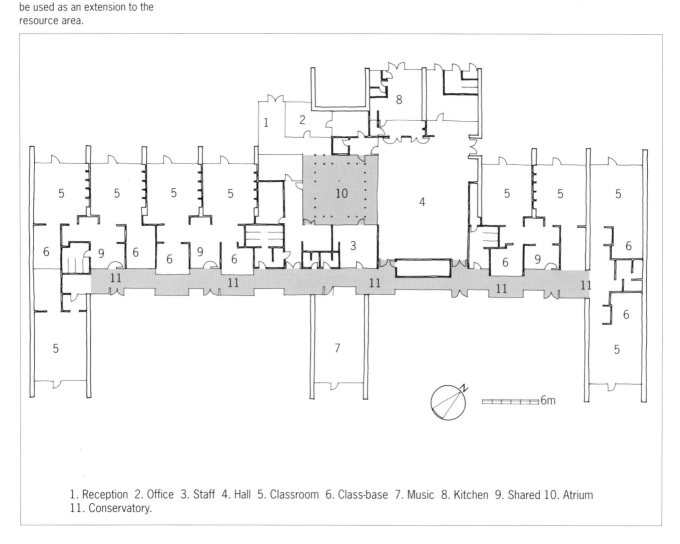

1. Reception 2. Office 3. Staff 4. Hall 5. Classroom 6. Class-base 7. Music 8. Kitchen 9. Shared 10. Atrium 11. Conservatory.

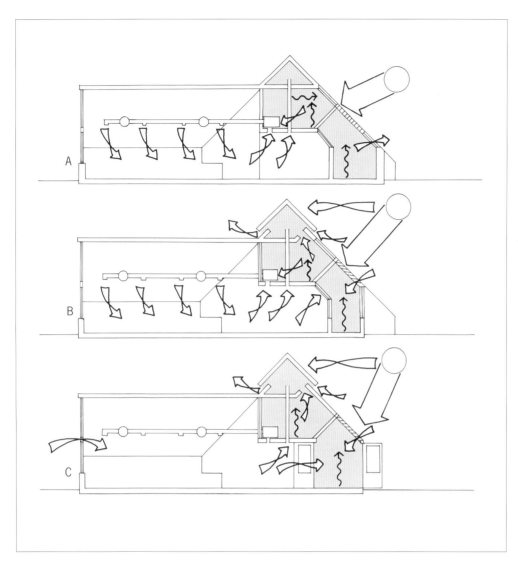

The high pitched roofs have eaves less than 2 m above ground level, the idea being to provide an appropriate scale for the children in the classrooms. Glazing to the conservatory and atrium is acrylic-coated twin-walled polycarbonate. North walls of the classrooms are timber framed, with asbestos cement board infill panels, insulation and plywood internal panels. The internal sloping soffits are formed with softwood battens laid over fire-retardant glass-fibre curtaining.

There is concrete paving over the slabs in the atrium and conservatory.

The roof has asbestos-cement slates.

Passive features

The conservatory was designed to provide pre-heated ventilation air for the classrooms during the heating season and to generate natural ventilation through these spaces in the summer through the unsealed eaves. Internal blinds in the conservatory prevent excessive temperatures being attained.

Heating and ventilation

Under the intended design conditions, during summer, the ventilation rates in the classrooms were only one quarter of the $30m^3$/person/hour required by Design Note 17. The only way of achieving adequate ventilation is to open the emergency exit doors in the north gables of the classrooms, because there are no openable windows. The north gable vents are also difficult to operate. In practice, the natural summer ventilation operates by cross-ventilation, with both the sets of classroom doors into the conservatory and to outside left open, rather than by the stack effect as was originally intended.

There is control of the heating and the

provision of fresh air to each classroom by independent ducted warm air heaters located at high level in the conservatory. The boilers, tanks and control panel are also located there.

An objective of the design was to give the users control over their environment. Classroom temperature is controlled by a knob marked 'warmer/cooler' and mechanical ventilation is achieved by a button marked 'fresh air', which switches from a full recirculation mode to a mix of pre-heated fresh air and recirculated air, which reverts to recirculation after a time delay of about 30 minutes.

The winter pre-heating mode with vitiated air from the classrooms drawn into the conservatory and recirculated to the classroom introduces little fresh air and tends to result in poor air quality.

Lighting

The southeast facing conservatory contributes to the daylighting of the teaching spaces adjacent to it, but all of the classrooms, except two, rely on north lighting for a large proportion of their natural light.

The daylighting of the hall and classrooms is not good, with glare from the windows in the classrooms causing excessive contrast to the whiteboard on the window wall.

Energy

The saving in natural gas consumption due to solar energy gain taken from the conservatory has been estimated to be 35%.

Amenity

The staff had an unfavourable view of the air quality in the classrooms and would have liked external openable windows. It was felt that the conservatory was frequently too cold in winter.

The conservatory would have been more useful if it had been wider, to accommodate practical activities in milder weather.

Energy and Building Statistics

Actual Annual Energy Consumption
Gas   79,861 kWh
Electricity   18,785 kWh
Total   98,646 kWh

Estimated catering consumption:
Gas   29700 kWh
Electricity   4620 kWh

Actual Annual Primary Energy Consumption:
= 174 kWh/m^2(corrected for region but not to national 20 year DD average and to exclude catering)

Number of pupil places: 220
Gross floor area: 835m^2 excluding unheated conservatories
Area of unheated conservatory and atrium: 200m^2

Building Cost: £371,011
External works: £39,239
Base date: March 1983
BNC/GFA: £444.32/m^2
Completed in 1984.

Consultants for passive solar design

N. Baker, Martin Centre, Cambridge.

Client

Hampshire Councy Council.

Architecture

D. Goodwin, Hampshire County Council Architects Dept.

Building Services Engineering

Fuller & Partners.

Conclusions

The solar heating strategy is effective in energy saving. However there are a number of design faults which prevent satisfactory environmental operation.

References

G.Nelson, 'What's the use of Atria?', Architects Journal, 20 Nov. 1984.

N.Baker, 'The Use of Passive Solar Gains for the Preheating of Ventilation Air', ETSU-S-1142, prepared for the Energy Technology Support Unit, Harwell, Oxfordshire, 1985.

D.U.Hawkes & R.Barbrook, 'Energetic Design - Netley Infants School', Architects Journal, 22 June 1988, p.31-49.

'Netley Abbey Infants' School, Energy Performance Assessment', Energy Technology Support Unit, Harwell, Oxfordshire, 1993.

South facing conservatory

Interior of conservatory showing air handling plant at high level. The conservatory is designed to pre-heat the ventilation air.

Newlands Junior School

Location

Dungell's Lane, Yately, Hampshire. The site is in an urban residential area, with existing oak and silver birch trees. An objective of the design was to retain the character of the existing heathland.

Design

The school is one of the first Hampshire designs to use the section to provide daylighting and ventilation to a deep plan.

Form

A small, unheated atrium connects the two blocks and provides an entrance. It is effectively 'gained space', helping to reduce heat losses from the spaces adjacent to it. The main teaching areas are in the southerly block of the building and the hall, plant room, staff room and kitchen are in the north block.

Construction

The atrium is a very lightweight structure.

The roof is tiled. Internally the roof trusses are exposed and those at the gable ends are glazed.

Plan of Newlands Junior School. The small, unheated atrium connects the two parts of the school and is effectively 'gained space', simultaneously helping to reduce heat losses from the spaces adjacent to it.

6m

1. Reception 2. Office 3. Staff 4. Hall 5. Classroom 6. Class-base 7. Resource 8. Music 9. Kitchen
10. Shared 11. Atrium

Passive features

The effect of the atrium in reducing heat losses from the building is only 7% of the total, according to Hawkes (1983). However, 56% of the wall area of the teaching spaces adjacent to it is glazed and it has been estimated that the atrium saves 23% of the heat loss which would otherwise occur if this space was open to the sky.

One problem noted was that during winter when the atrium became very cold, draughts of cold air from this space could enter the classrooms if the opening and shutting of doors was not strictly controlled. Overheating in the summer was not considered a problem as long as the ridge vents in the roof of the atrium were opened early in the morning. The east/west orientation of the atrium was considered to promote a good through draught if the doors were left open.

The manually-controlled vents in the ridge of the atrium are difficult to shut rapidly and rain can enter this space if a storm suddenly occurs. The atrium does not provide solar-heated air to the rest of the building.

The teaching areas face south and benefit from direct gains during the heating season. Eaves' overhangs on the southerly glazing reduce the solar gains and overheating during the summer.

Heating and ventilation

Summer temperatures are controlled by natural cross ventilation, high thermal capacity materials, and the use of internal blinds. The provision of a heated corridor at one end of the atrium facilitates internal circulation between all teaching spaces on cold days.

Heating is by a gas-fired boiler and radiator system.

Lighting

The two halves of the building are each covered by a pitched roof. These have glazed gable ends above the height of the eaves, and central ridge rooflights. Thus the spaces are substantially daylit, thereby reducing the need for artificial lighting.

Energy

The building is well insulated. A heat-recovery system in the kitchen is used to help provide hot water.

Sankey Diagram showing the energy supply to, and the consumption by the school

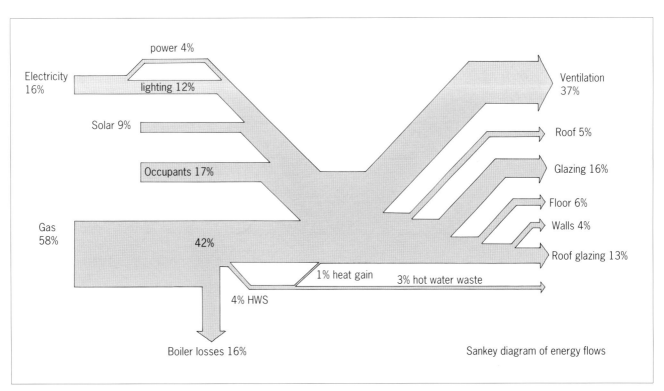

Sankey diagram of energy flows

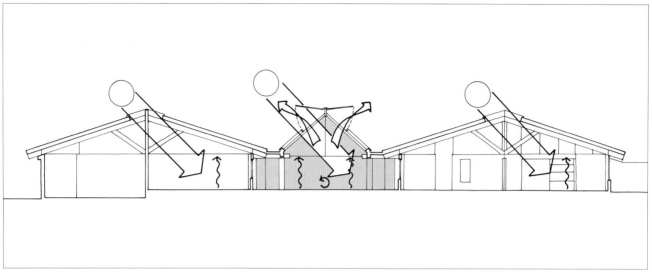

Section showing the opening ridge vents in the atrium. These allow warm air to be vented from the space below, thereby preventing discomfort to the occupants.

Amenity

The atrium is a popular feature of the school and is used for craft activities, as a waiting area for parents at the end of the school day, and as circulation space. It was not regarded as an extension of classroom space, although the classrooms open onto it. A feature of the atrium is a pond with surrounding tropical plants.

Energy and Building Statistics

Calculated Annual Primary Energy Consumption: 174 kWh/m²

Actual Annual Primary Energy Consumption: 130 kWh/m² (corrected from region and annual degree days to national 20 year DD average and to exclude catering)

Gross floor area: 910m² excluding conservatory
Unheated glazed area: 65m²
Teaching area: 722m²
Number of pupil places: 280, aged 5 to 11

BNC: £188,834 excluding external works
External works: £41,654
Base date: 2nd Quarter 1977
BNC/gross floor area: £207.51/m²
Completed in 1980.

Client

Hampshire County Council.

Architecture

Hampshire County Council Architects Department, M. Perkins (job architect), H. B. Eaton (directing architect).

Building Services Engineering

Adams Green and Partners.

Structural Engineering

Anthony Hunt Associates.

Conclusions

This school was the first application of a central atrium in a Hampshire school. It proved popular and atria were subsequently included in future designs.

References

Anon., 'Education', Architectural Review, January 1980, p.l0.

A. Le Cuyer, 'Public Panache', Architects Journal, 11 May 1981, p.771.

Anon., 'Hampshire Architecture', Academy Editions, London 1984.

G. Nelson, 'Schools as a Resource, 5. What's the Use of Atria?' Architects Journal, 28th November 1984, p.73-76.

D. Hawkes, 'Atria and Conservatories, 1 Introduction and Case Study'. Architects Journal, 11th May 1983, p.67-70.

D. Hawkes, 'Building Study - Yately Newlands Primary School, Hampshire', Architects Journal, 24th June 1981, p.1199-1214.

The atrium roof is visible from the main school entrance (i.e. the northeast)

The atrium also serves as a lobby area for the main entrance

Perronet Thompson Comprehensive School

Location

Wawne Road, North Bransholme, Hull, Humberside. The school is located on an open site and serves a large estate of local authority rented housing.

Design

A sports hall, gymnasium, public library and community facilities are located under an 80 metre-long central barrel vault. At the north end, a semi-circular block contains a theatre and the south end features a 4-storey inclined glazed wall. The classrooms are located around six courtyards, three on each side of the central vaulted structure. Each of these features a glazed central courtyard.

Construction

The outer skin of the barrel vault is of polycarbonate. The central 4-storey high unheated public courtyard is open to this outer skin. A second inner skin over the gymnasium and sports hall was originally

Plans of Perronet Thompson Comprehensive School.

Above. The first floor plan showing the lightwells to both the classroom atria and the central areas.

Below. The ground floor plan showing the location of the classrooms around six internal courtyards.

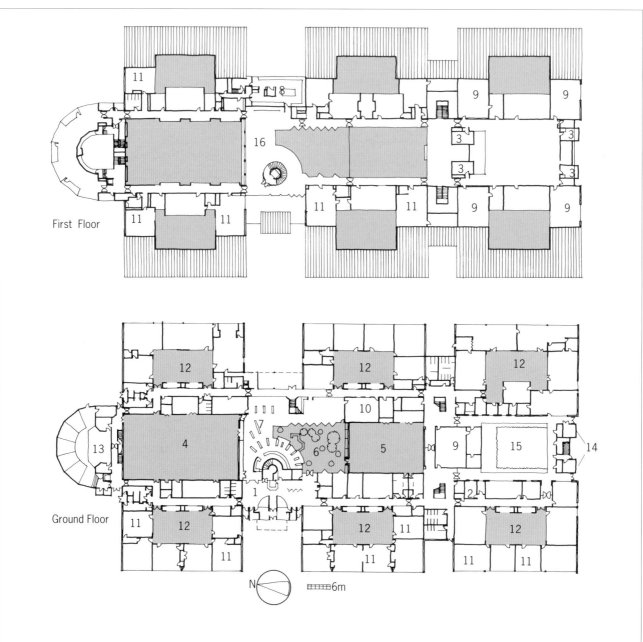

1. Reception 2. Office 3. Staff 4. Sports Hall 5. Gym 6. Atrium 7. Community Library 8. Kitchen 9. Laboratory
10. Computer 11. Classroom 12. Shared courtyard 13. Drama 14. Conservatory 15. External courtyard 16. Dining

composed of 5 layers of crosslinked pvc. The translucent inner skin was intended to provide a diffuse source of natural light without the distraction to sport of direct sunlight. Originally it provided adequate daylight without the need to switch on the lights. However by 1992, four years after completion, due to migration of the upper bronze tinted layer into the lower layers and heat degradation, it had discoloured and become brittle and the SON lighting was required all the time. The panels were therefore replaced by polycarbonate sheets applied in a double layer - an outer 8 mm bronze tinted skin and an inner 16 mm triple walled skin (similar to that used for the classroom atria). The original natural light levels have been restored and overall insulation levels improved.

The school has a high thermal mass and high levels of insulation. The main building is compact in form; being designed with a minimal external envelope (perimeter walls are single storey in height) constructed around a steel frame with high mass buff-textured blockwork with an insulated cavity (having a U-value = $0.4W/m^{2\circ}C$).

The general construction of the roof (excluding spine and service areas), is highly insulated (e.g. U-value = $0.3W/m^{2\circ}C$). It has a profiled sheet-steel outer layer which, with the steel purlins, is treated internally with a site applied anti-condensation coating.

The glazing over the six classroom atria has an outer 6 mm thick single, clear polycarbonate-layer, separated by the 250 mm depth of the purlins, from an inner triple polycarbonate layer of 16 mm overall thickness. Only two-thirds of this roof area is glazed: this reduces heat gains and losses whilst not reducing significantly the borrowed light to the adjoining classrooms.

Passive features

The high mass construction is intended to increase the thermal storage capacity of the building and thus to dampen swings in temperature.

There are four main features subject to solar gains; three are purely passive and one active or hybrid:

(a) An unheated 4-storey high atrium under the central barrel vault, intended primarily for community use.
This space has not been designed to take advantage of solar gain.

(b) The six unheated atria provide shared teaching areas during most of the year except for about 10 weeks from January to mid-March, and five of them double as assembly and social spaces for each year group. The sixth is used as a craft, design and technology workshop for project work. Air heated by solar gains in the courtyards may be used to heat or ventilate adjacent classrooms. This heat gain supplements the gas-fired warm air heating. Temperature and occupancy sensors are installed to use the solar heated air to best advantage via a system of dampers and fans. Some of these classrooms surrounding the atria have no direct natural lighting or natural ventilation, which is less than ideal.

(c) A 4-storey high south facing wall, its glazing sloping at about 50 degrees. The wall was not designed to exploit its solar energy potential and solar controls are absent from this feature. Behind the glass at ground floor level is a conservatory which provides an obviously useful extension to the adjacent science area. Above it are 2-storey high staff resource rooms. Some problems of overheating have been experienced in the two staff rooms, in spite of the use of solar glass, and a scheme of air extraction and blinds has been proposed or, alternatively, the replacing of a proportion of the glazing with metal insulated panels. The amount of useful floor area is not great for the volume enclosed and the steep angle of the solar wall restricts the use of the space immediately behind it.

(d) Roof-space collectors above the centrally placed sports hall and gymnasium. As these rely on mechanical equipment for their usefulness, they should be regarded as primarily active or

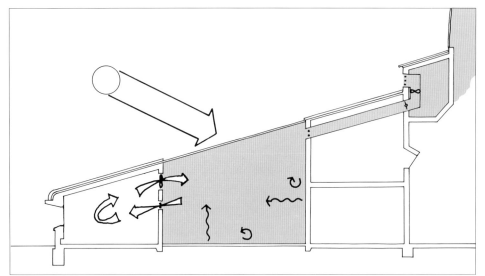

Schematic section showing autumn/spring operation of the ventilation system. Air heated by solar gains in the six external courtyards may be used to heat or ventilate adjacent classroom areas.

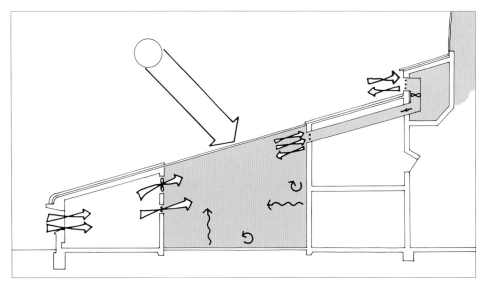

Schematic section showing summer operation. High level ventilation fans operate automatically to stabilise courtyard temperatures when solar gains are high. Classroom windows may be opened and this provides induced through ventilation as required.

hybrid features.

The insulated inner barrel vault serves to trap air in what is effectively a roof-space collector. During periods of solar gain and low ambient temperature this air is used to heat the main body of the school and is circulated by air handling units.

Heating and ventilation

A combination of radiators, convectors and air handling units provide heating. The atria blocks are zoned independently of each other and of the main central zone to allow for partial use. Heating and lighting to the classrooms is controlled by ultrasonic occupancy sensors.

The main external doors and following lobby doors are sensor driven. The two sets of doors are directly in line with a very short path between them. Whilst the

One of the six unheated courtyards in the classroom blocks

design intention was undoubtedly to reduce the energy consumption by having self-closing doors, the close proximity of the two sets of doors necessarily results in them always being open simultaneously. The situation is at its worst during the main periods of entry when, according to staff, the doors are never shut. Simply increasing the distance between the doors would not prevent this occuring at peak times when there is a continuous flow of children entering the building.

All the core areas of the school (including the sports hall, gymnasium, dining areas and library) are served from individual air handling units, through ceiling mounted diffusers. The AHUs have been installed within the roof to take solar warmed air from the huge glazed vault to the receiving areas. The design intention was that each system be controlled via 3 stage modulation controllers as stated below:

Stage 1: During the winter months (i.e. for cold, cloudy, ambient conditions), heated air is provided to the zones via their individual heater batteries.

Stage 2: During mid-season (ie. under cold, sunny, ambient conditions), the solar gain picked up within the barrel vault is transferred via flexible ductwork as pre-heat to the heater batteries.

Stage 3: During the summer period (i.e. when hot, sunny ambient conditions apply), the heater batteries are switched off and any heating requirement is obtained via the solar heated air alone. Once internal temperature limits are reached within the space, dampers turn down the amount of air from the barrel vault and the proportion of fresh air from the external louvres is increased.

Amenity

The sports hall, gym and community library are in use all year except for statutory holidays. There is considerable amenity value in the central daylit spaces.

Architecture and Building Services Engineering

Humberside County Council Property Services Department.

Structural Engineers

Oscar Faber Partnership.

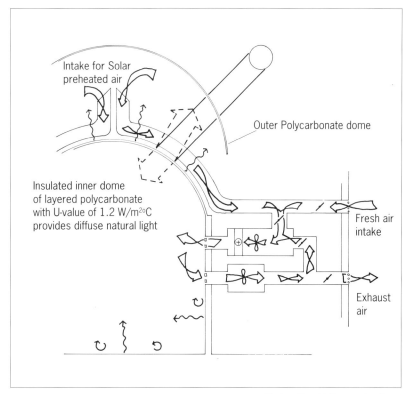

Air handling Units supply all core areas including the sports hall, gymnasium, dining areas and library.

Community atrium open to the polycarbonate outer skin of the roof [Humberside C.C.]

Conclusions

The six atria in the classroom blocks provide additional teaching space in clement weather and, perhaps more importantly, social spaces used at break times.

The futuristic design is popular with the children. It received a Commendation in the 1989 British Steel Design Awards and a North East Region Gas Energy Management Award in 1988.

West elevation

The sports hall is daylit via the
translucent roof
[Humberside C.C.]

The south facing glazed wall

Energy

The primary energy consumption of 270kWh/(m² gross floor area), excluding catering, corrected for Degree days and normal school hours, is slightly higher than the design target quoted in Department for Education Design Note 17 for primary energy consumption of 238kWh/m² (which also excludes catering).

The overall hours of use for the school are approximately 2676 compared with a normal secondary school figure of 1660 hours. This gives the correction factor for normal secondary school hours of use of 0.62. The school degree days for the 1993/94 were 2259 compared with the 20 year Degree Day average of 2094 used in the DN17 calculation, giving a correction factor of 0.93.

Energy and Building Statistics

Gross floor area: 9,947m² excluding the unheated areas (except 200m² for circulation) but including the public library and community facilities.
Unheated glazed area: 1010m²
(exc. 200m² for circulation)
Number of pupil places: 1200

Actual Annual Energy Consumption for 1993/94:
Electricity day rate   415,931kWh
Electricity night rate   63,867kWh
Gas excluding catering   1,868,115kWh
Gas for catering (estimate)   146,600kWh
Total excluding catering   2,347,913kWh

Conversion to Primary Energy Units(corrected for normal secondary school hours of use and from region and annual degree days to national 20 year DD average and excluding catering):
Electricity   1,113,849kWh
Gas   1,568,114kWh
Total   2,681,963kWh

Total Annual Primary Energy Consumption
= 270kWh/m²GFA

Building Net Cost: £4,252,997 excluding external works
External works: £544,736
Base date: June 1986
BNC/gross floor area: £427.57/m²
Completed: 1988.

References

Bunn, R., 1988, 'Comprehensive Engineering', Building Services, Vol. 10, No. 12, December 1988, p.21-25.

Williams, A., Perronet Thompson School, Building, January 1989, p.45-52.

St Peter's Primary School Coggeshall

Location

Myneer Park, Coggeshall, Colchester, Essex, CO6 1YU, 51.8N 0.5W.

Design

This is a split-level building with open-plan classroom areas on the lower level of the school facing southeast and southwest. The upper level of the school houses administration and specialist teaching areas.

Form

A one metre step in the section separates the hall, administration and specialist teaching areas on the higher-level from the classrooms on the south-east and southwest. The circulation runs in an L-shape between these two areas and around the double height hall. The circulation area has roof glazing. Most of the inner walls onto this circulation are substantially glazed, so allowing borrowed light into the deep-plan teaching areas from the circulation corridor. The audio/visual room and deputy head's office are located at first floor level over the main circulation route, and there are balconies at this level overlooking the hall and the circulation route.

Passive features

The school has extensive glazing, which provides daylighting to the rear of the classroom areas and illuminates the administration circulation spaces. There are few criticisms of this building. One concern expressed is excessive solar gains via the glazing during the summer. Another relates to the remoteness of the switches for electric lighting to some of the teaching areas.

Plan of St Peter's School Coggeshall. The classrooms and the hall are separated by the circulation area, which runs in an L-shape between the two areas. The deputy-head's office and audio visual room are located on the first floor.

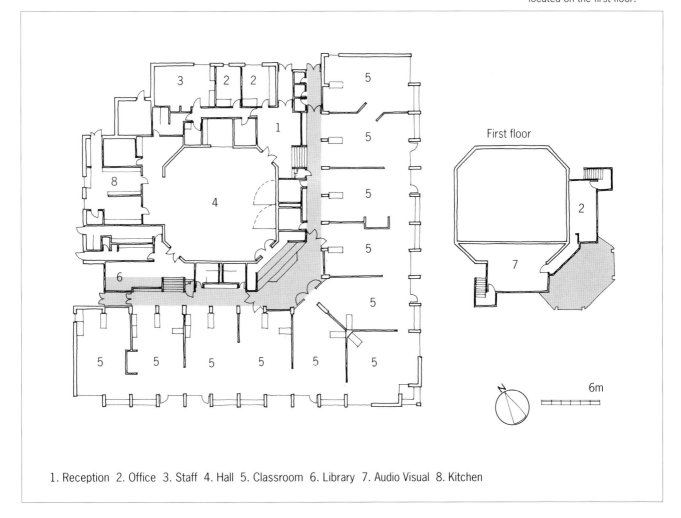

First floor

6m

1. Reception 2. Office 3. Staff 4. Hall 5. Classroom 6. Library 7. Audio Visual 8. Kitchen

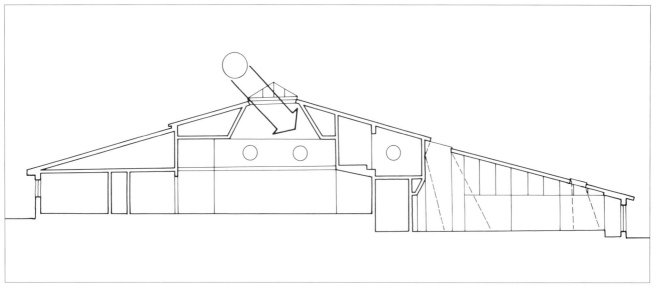

Section showing the split level arrangement of the school. The circulation areas, adjacent to the classrooms, have roof glazing. The inner walls onto this circulation are glazed, so allowing borrowed daylight into the deep-plan teaching areas.

Lighting

A glazed pyramid rooflight lets light into the hall.

Amenity

The building is popular, very comfortable in the winter, and considered to be a good working environment. The head teacher was involved in the design of the building from an early stage.

Client

Essex County Council.

Architecture

B. Page, County Architect's Dept. Essex County Council.

Environmental Engineering

B. King, County Architect's Dept. Essex County Council.

Energy and Building Statistics

Calculated Annual Primary Energy Consumption
= 141.3kWh/m^2

Actual Annual Primary Energy Consumption
= 98 kWh/m^2 (corrected from region and annual degree days to national 20 year DD average and to exclude catering)

Gross floor area: 1149m^2
Teaching area: 780m^2
Number of pupil places: 330

Building Net Cost (BNC): £389,643 excluding external works
External works: £76,037

Base date: 2nd Quarter 1984
BNC/gross floor area: £339.11/m^2
Completed in 1988.

Southeast elevation

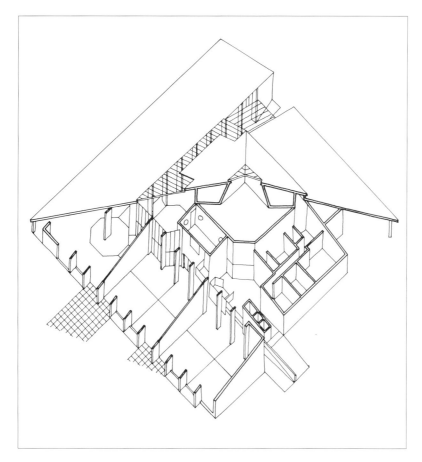

Axonometric of the school with cut away showing the central hall and classrooms. The extensive glazing provides daylighting to the rear of the classroom areas and illuminates the circulation areas.

Interior showing borrowed light to classrooms from the corridor

Swanlea Secondary School

Location

Brady Street, Whitechapel, London. The school is in the east end of London. It is on the corner of two streets and is bounded on the north by a burial ground with some fine trees and on the west by an underground railway.

Design

In order to provide good communication between subject areas the school is designed around a main street with circulation by means of high-level walkways, bridge links and a disabled access lift. By careful fire-engineering the stairs at each end of the mall have not been enclosed in fire compartments, which eases the access beween levels.

Form

The teaching spaces are on three storeys on the north side of the mall and two storeys on the south. The south facing slope of the roof over the mall takes up the difference in levels and also maximises solar gains. The building is constructed on a module equal to the classroom width of 8.1 metres. This is expressed externally by the classroom setbacks and the repeating crest shaped slopes of the classroom roofs.

Construction

Bored cast in-situ piled foundations support a ventilated suspended ground floor slab. The walls are of loadbearing blockwork clad with bricks or cladding panels with insulated cavities. The street elevations are mainly in yellow London stock bricks, similar to existing local buildings. Internal walls are largely of plastered loadbearing blockwork with extensive glazing onto the mall. Blockwork partitions provide the robustness, fire resistance and acoustic separation needed and are an economical form of construction. Pre-cast gutters provide fire stability to the compartment walls.

Upper floors were formed with pre-cast shuttering with integral void formers to provide service routes and reduce weight. The curved roofs to the classrooms are built up from profiled aluminium sheet with standing seams carried on curved steel T-sections.

Passive features

The mall is glazed with special glass panels. These are hermetically sealed and double glazed. They incorporate purpose designed 'Okasolar' reflective glass prismatic strips set at predetermined angles. The angles of the prisms are adjusted depending on the location of the glass panel on the roof slope. This is because the slope of the roof gets steeper towards the bottom. The angle is chosen to reflect the majority of the sunshine in summer and to transmit the majority in winter. The angle depends on the altitude of the sun in summer and the angle that the glazing makes with the horizontal. The glass prisms are reflective and a form of fixed shading device. The glass is largely self-cleaning as the minimum slope is 15 degrees.

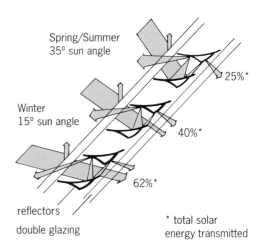

Summer
55° sun angle

Spring/Summer
35° sun angle

Winter
15° sun angle

25%*

40%*

62%*

reflectors
double glazing

* total solar
energy transmitted

Detail section through 'Okasolar' double glazing

The mall is unheated except for passive solar gains and gains from the adjoining classrooms. Significantly, there have been no complaints that the mall is too hot or too cold. It therefore provides a useful thermal buffer space. The end walls are fully glazed as is the opening onto the south exhibition courtyard. In the heating season, when the temperature of the air in

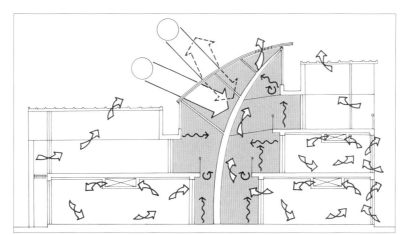

Environmental section through the central mall

the mall reaches 20°C it is used as a pre-heated supply for the mechanical ventilation system serving the classrooms. In summer, overheating of the mall is prevented by thermostatic opening of the fire ventilators located in the top section of the sloping roof.

Heating and ventilation

Both the cavity walls and the roof are well insulated with U-values around 0.3W/m²°C, much lower than required by the Building Regulations. The larger classrooms, laboratories and technology spaces are provided with mechanical ventilation. A scheme of natural ventilation using the stack effect generated in the mall was considered but was found to conflict with the necessary fire and acoustic separation. However, heat reclaim using plate heat exchangers (for low maintenance) and the use of solar pre-heated air from the central mall make the ventilation system energy efficient.

Out of hours use of part of the building is easy with heating-on times of four separate heating zones controlled from a central computer. Also a separate boilerhouse serves the catering and sports area. The main boilerhouse serves the rest of the school. The heating system has weather compensation, optimum start and radiators are fitted with thermostatic valves. Hot water is provided by local hot water generators, except for the kitchen and shower rooms which are served from their own boiler plant.

Lighting

The maximum amount of daylight is admitted to all areas. Classrooms are lit from two sides; from the main view windows and from the clerestory glazing under the raised edges of the classroom roofs. Light is also borrowed from the central mall.

High frequency fluorescent lighting is used in most areas. In the classrooms a two stage switching arrangement controls each of two sets of bulbs in each luminaire so that the lighting can be adjusted to suit the level of daylight available. A central time control enables all classroom lights to be switched off at break or lunch time. This has proved cost effective in other schools.

Energy

The building has predicted primary energy consumption figures based on the DN17 calculation, which are much lower than the target values. The energy efficiency is due in large part to the simple heating and lighting controls aided by the unheated passive solar mall.

Energy and Building Statistics

Calculated Annual Energy Consumption in primary energy units = 148 kWh/m²
Calculated Energy Design Value in primary energy units = 96W/m² (compared to DN17 target of 120W/m²)
Teaching area: 5092m²
Gross floor area (excluding the central mall): 9,023m²
Area of unheated mall: 1,486m²
Number of pupil places: 1050

Building Net Cost (BNC): £6,981,800 excluding external works
External works: £580,000
Base date: 4th Quarter 1993
BNC/gross floor area: £773.78/m²
Completed in August 1993
Public sector tender price index: 249.

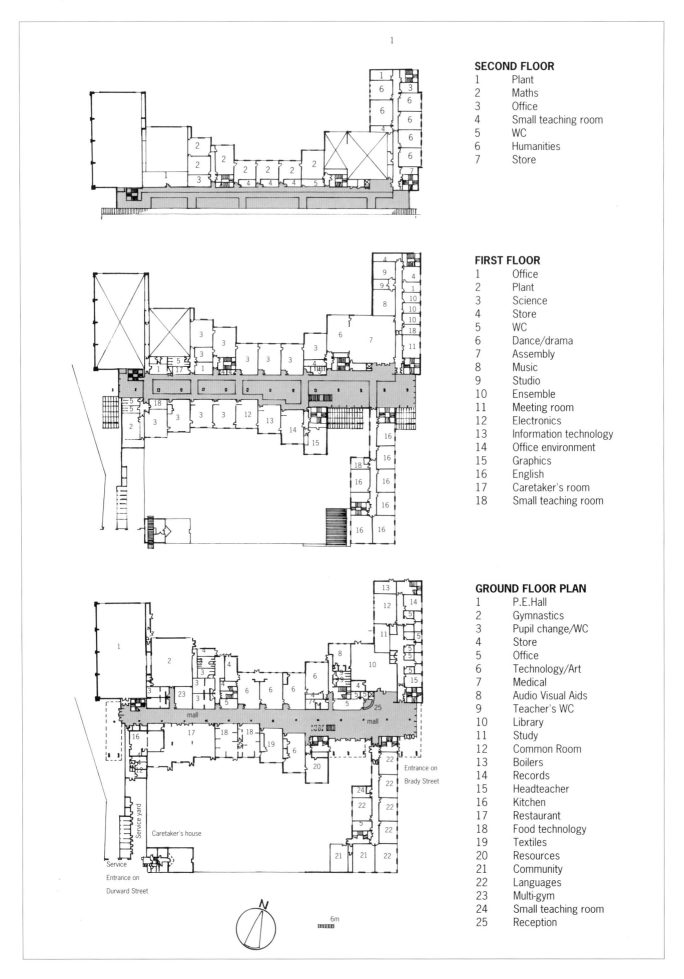

SECOND FLOOR

1	Plant
2	Maths
3	Office
4	Small teaching room
5	WC
6	Humanities
7	Store

FIRST FLOOR

1	Office
2	Plant
3	Science
4	Store
5	WC
6	Dance/drama
7	Assembly
8	Music
9	Studio
10	Ensemble
11	Meeting room
12	Electronics
13	Information technology
14	Office environment
15	Graphics
16	English
17	Caretaker's room
18	Small teaching room

GROUND FLOOR PLAN

1	P.E.Hall
2	Gymnastics
3	Pupil change/WC
4	Store
5	Office
6	Technology/Art
7	Medical
8	Audio Visual Aids
9	Teacher's WC
10	Library
11	Study
12	Common Room
13	Boilers
14	Records
15	Headteacher
16	Kitchen
17	Restaurant
18	Food technology
19	Textiles
20	Resources
21	Community
22	Languages
23	Multi-gym
24	Small teaching room
25	Reception

Entrance on
Brady Street

Service yard

Caretaker's house

Service

Entrance on
Durward Street

N

6m

Amenity

Community use of the school has been considered as part of the design. The sports and catering facilities are separately zoned for heating, allowing economical letting. A creche and community rooms are provided adjacent to the language department. The landscaping provides paved play areas and formal gardens. An ecological garden forms the focus of the southern courtyard and the small courtyard directly accessible from the mall is intended as an exhibition area.

Client and project management

Bethnal Green Neighbourhood Project Management, London Borough of Tower Hamlets Education Department.

Architecture

The Percy Thomas Partnership.

Structural Engineers

YRM Anthony Hunt Associates.

Services Engineers

Whitby and Bird.

Thermal and smoke modelling

Design Flow Solutions.

Fire Engineering

Colt International Ltd.

Second floor classroom [Charlotte Wood]

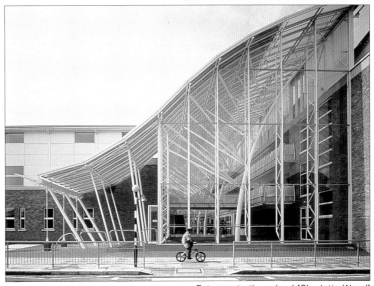

Entrance to the school [Charlotte Wood]

View from the south [Charlotte Wood]

References

Architects Journal, October 1993.

The passive solar mall showing the curved tapering circular hollow section support columns and the fire ventilators at the top of the sloping roof [Charlotte Wood]

Roach Vale Primary School

Location

Roach Vale, Parsons Heath, Colchester, Essex, CO4 3EZ.

Design

The school was built using Essex County Council's Modular Component Building (MCB) system.

Form

The school is of cruciform plan. Eight teaching bases are arranged in pairs and grouped around the courtyard. The hall, kitchen and administrative areas are linked to the teaching block by an entrance lobby.

Construction

The building has an aerated concrete, load bearing, pre-cast skin with glazing areas of 25% or less.

Passive features

One of the five air-to-air heat pumps which heat this school uses pre-heated air taken from the covered courtyard as its input source.

The glazed central courtyard enables heat to be reclaimed from vitiated air from the surrounding teaching areas together with solar gains through the pyramidal translucent roofing. The controlled environment areas of this school are heated in winter and cooled in summer by the roof mounted heat pumps.

The external workspaces are each covered with four translucent glass fibre pyramids supported off a central column. They were originally planned to be semi-enclosed to provide some shelter but have in fact been left with open sides.

Plan of Roach Vale Primary School. Four pairs of teaching bases are arranged in a cruciform plan around the central courtyard. The hall, kitchen and administrative areas are linked to the teaching block by an entrance lobby.

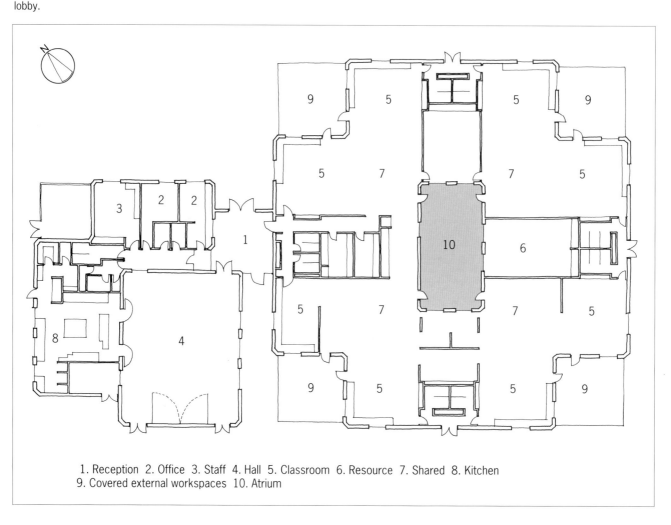

1. Reception 2. Office 3. Staff 4. Hall 5. Classroom 6. Resource 7. Shared 8. Kitchen
9. Covered external workspaces 10. Atrium

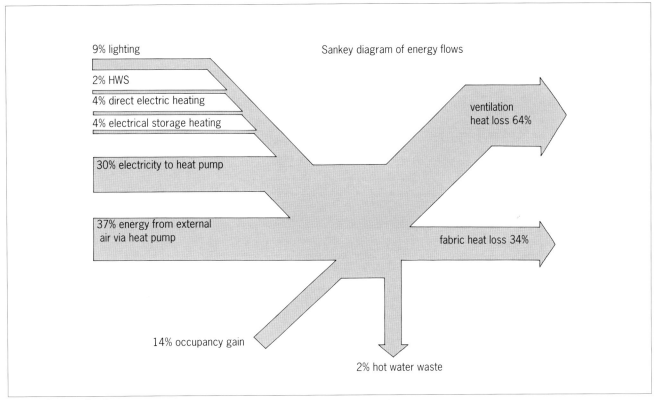

9% lighting

2% HWS

4% direct electric heating

4% electrical storage heating

30% electricity to heat pump

37% energy from external air via heat pump

14% occupancy gain

Sankey diagram of energy flows

ventilation heat loss 64%

fabric heat loss 34%

2% hot water waste

Sankey diagram showing energy supply and consumption of the school

Schematic section showing the operation of the heat pumps. Above. Winter operation of the roof mounted heat pumps. Below. Summer operation of the roof mounted heat pumps.

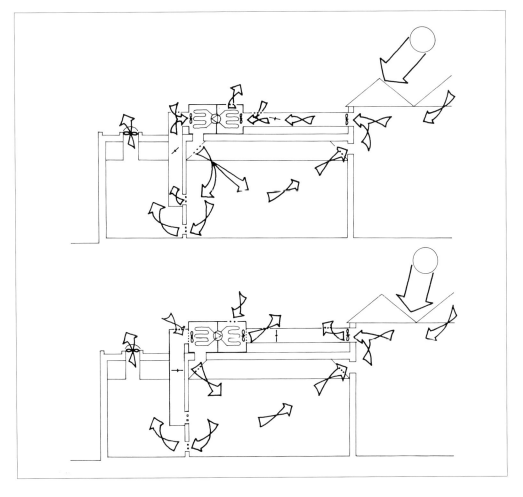

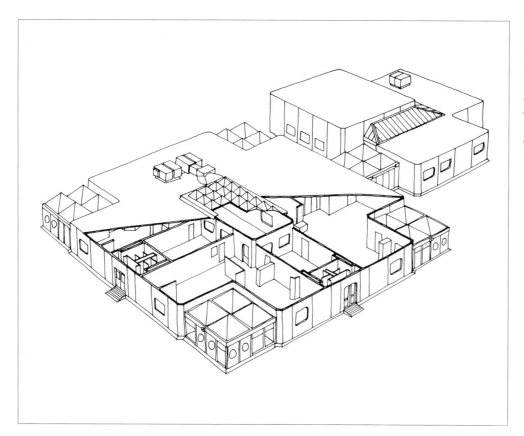

Isometric perspective with cut away showing the general configuration of the class-rooms and central courtyard. Roof glazing comprises translucent pyramids. External workspace corner areas are shown semi-enclosed as originally planned.

Heating and ventilation

It is thought to be the first school with a purpose-designed solar assisted heat pump in the UK.

Hot water is provided by local electric heaters rated at 3kW with a 44 litre capacity.

Energy and Building Statistics

Calculated Annual Energy Consumption Value in Primary Energy Units = 258kWh/m²

Actual Annual Energy Consumption:
86/87 electricity   103586 kWh
87/88 electricity   98798 kWh

Estimated catering consumption:
Electricity   15930 kWh

Actual Average Primary Energy Consumption Value (corrected from region and annual degree days to national 20 year DD average and to exclude catering) = 274 kWh/m²

Gross floor area: 1119m² excluding 40m² atrium
Teaching area: 673m²
Unheated glazed area: 40m²
Number of pupil places: 295

Building Net Cost (BNC): £225,942 including external works
Base date: 1st Quarter 1977
BNC/gross floor area: £201.91/m².

Client

Essex County Council.

Architecture and Building Services Engineering

County Architect's Dept., Essex County Council.

Monitoring

Performance monitored by Electricity Council Research Centre, Capenhurst.

References

G. Kasabov (Editor), 1979, 'Buildings : The Key to Energy Conservation', Royal Institute of British Architects, London, UK.

I. P. Duncan and D. U. Hawkes, 'Passive Solar Design in Non-domestic Buildings', ETSU Report ETSU-S-lllOD, Harwell, Oxfordshire, UK.

P. Page, 1981, 'School Buildings - Essex County Council Architect's Department', The Architecture of Energy (Hawkes and Owers Eds.), Construction Press, p.195-215.

Anon, 1980, Energy Blueprint No.7: 'School's heat pumps teach vital energy lessons', Architects Journal, 12 March 1980.

Thorpe Bay High School

Location

Southchurch Boulevard,
Southend-on-Sea, Essex, SS2 4UY.

Design

This is an example of a school in which passive solar features have been adopted as part of a remodelling and refurbishment of buildings dating from the late 1950s. Prior to the refurbishment, the Dowsett High School for Girls provided 4494 m² of teaching accommodation for 600 pupils. The school was then amalgamated with Southchurch Hall Boys School to form the co-educational comprehensive Thorpe Bay High School of 5548 m² for 900 pupils.

Form

The school buildings comprise four blocks placed on a northwest-southeast axis around a central courtyard. The blocks to the north and south are two storeys in height and the other two blocks of single storey construction. The latter blocks enclose a series of smaller courts and a courtyard.

In terms of energy efficiency, the adverse features of the original Dowsett School building were identified by Page (1983) as follows:
○ Pavilion planning with unprotected internal courtyards with high external wall-to-floor ratio.
○ Excessive amounts of glazing.
○ Unprotected external circulation areas leading to high infiltration rates.
○ Lack of zone control of heating.

Construction

The primary superstructure of the main blocks is built with a steel frame and lattice roof structure, an insulated deck roof, brick cavity walls and timber framed infill panels. These panels were recently replaced with a proprietary thermally broken aluminium section with gasketed windows.

Passive solar features

These features include glazed streets and courtyards as part of the refurbishment and remodelling. By the provision of glazed circulation areas and the enclosure of courtyards, the infiltration rates were reduced and the insulation of the fabric improved. These measures, plus a range of energy efficient techniques, have resulted in a building with energy consumption levels which do not exceed those of the former Dowsett School.

The glazed areas were carpeted, which led to enhanced temperatures during winter. However it also reduced the effectiveness of the floor slab as thermal mass and thus its ability to ameliorate temperature swings.

Heating and ventilation

In summer the extract fans provided could not cope with the build-up of heat in the glazed areas. The fans are too small and poorly located in the upstand of the glazed lantern roofs. Teachers described the summer environment of these areas as 'unbearable, airless, feeling of no oxygen, humid, sticky'. On hot days, the pupils would usually move to one of the playgrounds surrounding the school. Despite the teachers' efforts to leave doors open 'the air did not seem to move'.

Staff found the glazed corridor and courtyards cold in the winter, but the main problem in the school was that often the end doors of the glazed spaces would remain open, allowing free circulation, and this would create draughts. But, on the whole, they were not dissatisfied with the winter conditions and only half of the staff acknowledged that they could do with some background heating to 'take the edge away on some days'. A number of them thought that it would make the classroom warmer as well, but clearly their main concern seemed to be with the end doors, which should be enclosed in some kind of air-lock system to stop unpleasant draughts.

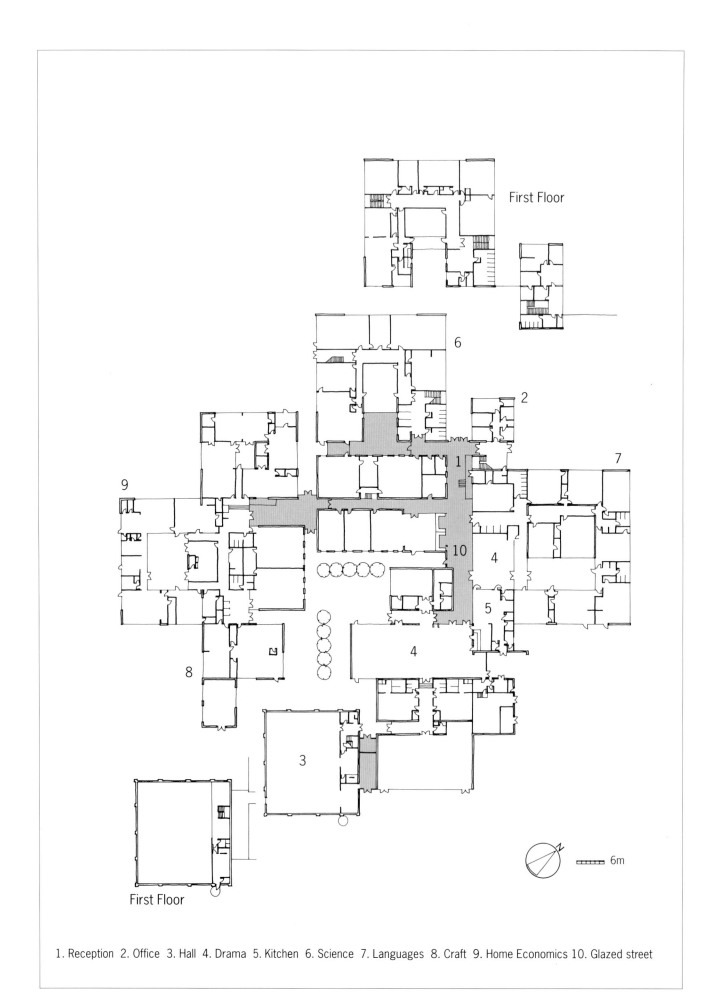

First Floor

First Floor

1. Reception 2. Office 3. Hall 4. Drama 5. Kitchen 6. Science 7. Languages 8. Craft 9. Home Economics 10. Glazed street

6m

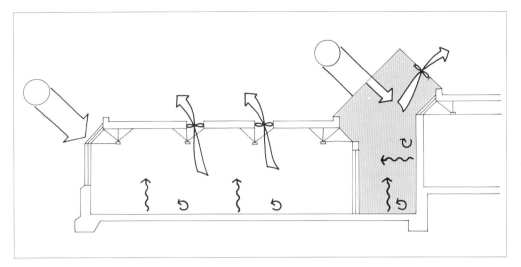

Schematic section showing the general arrangement of passive solar features, including the provision of glazed streets as part of the refurbishment of the school. Extract fans were provided to deal with solar gains in the glazed areas during the summer, but have proved inadequate.

Lighting

As the glazed areas of Thorpe Bay School were retrofitted, the teachers could compare the conditions in the school before and after the exercise. No comments were forthcoming that indicated either additional noise or noticeable loss of daylighting. Members of staff found the main areas of the building bright, airy, open and aesthetically pleasing.

The main glazed street looking west

Courtyard and glazed roofs of the streets

Energy

The original building had a heat load of 715kW. The new school has a larger floor area with a roughly equal calculated heat load of 706kW, and also a new sports hall with a 65kW heating load.

Energy and Building Statistics

Actual Annual Energy Consumption:

1986/87 electricity	On Peak	190012 kWh
	Off Peak	43736 kWh
	gas	1539304 kWh

1987/88 electricity	On Peak	187322 kWh
	Off Peak	51936 kWh
	gas	1295188 kWh

Estimated catering consumption:
Electricity   on peak   26100 kWh
Gas   167400 kWh

Actual Average Annual Primary Energy Consumption (corrected from region and annual degree days to national 20-year DD average and to exclude catering) = 344 kWh/m²

Gross floor area of extension: 1408m²
excluding 300m² glazed area
final school GFA: 7452m²

Teaching area of extension: 1054m²
final school teaching area: 5548m²
Unheated glazed area of extension: 300m²

Number of pupil places: 900 (remodelling and extension of former 600 pupil girls' school)

Building Net Cost (BNC):£486,225 excluding abnormals and external works
External works: £120,904
Base date: 2nd Quarter 1982
BNC/gross floor area: £345.33/m²
Completed and extended in 1983.

Amenity

The glazed corridor and courtyards were used primarily as a recreation and meeting area for the upper school and a playground for the lower school. A public address system played music in the recreation area (the choice of music being the pupils' own; the volume at which it was played being controlled by the teachers from the staffroom). The glazed courtyards were viewed as a successful social forum for the school.

Conclusions

This refurbishment shows the amenity and energy-saving values of covering courtyards and circulation routes between existing buildings. It also shows the necessity of providing adequate thermal mass and ventilation to prevent summer-time overheating and the need for adequate draft lobbies on external doors.

Client

Essex County Council.

Architecture and Building Services Engineering

County Architect's Dept., Essex County Council.

Consultant for passive solar design

Dr. A. Jones, Cranfield University (now of Environmental Design Simulations Ltd.)

References

A. Willis, 1984, 'Thorpe Bay High School', Report by the County Architect to the Education Committee, Essex County Council.

D. U. Hawkes, 1985, 'Courtyards : the case for enclosure'. Final report to Science and Engineering Research Council on Grant No. GR/C/53442, 1984.

P. A. Page, 'Towards a Better Understanding of Climate-Respecting Design', Proc. 2nd International PLEA Conference, Passive and Low Energy Architecture, Crete, Greece, 1983, p.15-27.

References

Anon., Design Note 17, 'Guidelines for Environmental Design and Fuel Conservation in Educational Buildings', Department of Education and Science, 1981.

Anon., 1933, 'The Orientation of Buildings', Royal Institute of British Architects, London, 1933.

Anon., 1985, 'The Refurbishment Potential in School Buildings', Energy Technology Support Unit Market Study No.4. Energy Publications, Energy Efficiency Office, 1985.

Baker, N., 1983, 'Atria and Conservatories, 2, Case Study 2', Architects Journal, Vol.177, No.20, 11 May 1983, p.67-69.

Baker, N., 1983, 'Atria and Conservatories, 3, Principles of Design', Architects Journal, Vol.177, No.21, 25 May 1983, p.67-70.

Baker, N., 1986, 'Atria and Conservatories', Proc. 2nd UK-ISES Conference, 'The Efficient Use of Energy in Buildings' (C46), Cranfield University, UK, Sept.1986, p.32-41.

Banham, R., 1969, 'The Architecture of the Well-Tempered Environment', The Architectural Press, London, p.280-289, 1969.

Barra, O. A. & Carratelli, E. P., 1979, 'A Theoretical Study of Laminar Free Convection in l-D Solar Induced Flows', Solar Energy, 23, p.211-215, 1979.

Bowman, N., 1982, 'Less Fuel at School', Architects Journal, 10 November 1982, p.85-88.

Buchanan, P., 1982, Architectural Review, July 1982, No.1025, Vol.CLXXII.

Commission of the European Communities, Building 2000, Volume 1, 'Schools, Laboratories and Universities, Sports and Educational Centres', Kluwer Academic Publishers, 1992, ISBN 0 7923 1501 4.

Crisp, V. H. C., Littlefair, P., Cooper, I. and McKennan G., 1988, 'Daylighting as a Passive Solar Energy Option', Final Report to the Energy Technology Support Unit, Contract No.ET/174/175/099. Building Research Establishment, Garston, Watford, 1988.

Curtis, D., 1988, 'Opportunities for the Use of Passive Solar Energy in Educational Buildings', Report No.17, Watt Committee on Energy, Passive Solar Energy in Buildings, Ed. P. O'Sullivan, Elsevier Applied Science Publishers, 1988, p.5-22.

Duncan, I. P. & Hawkes, D. U., 1983, 'Passive Solar Design in Non-domestic Buildings', Report to The Energy Technology Support Unit, Harwell, Oxfordshire, Report No. ETSU-S-lllOD, June 1983, p.114-115.

Frances, R., Field, J., Lloyd, N. and Rofe, Y., 1982, 'A study of potential applications for active solar heating in the non-domestic buildings sector'. ETSU Report ETSU-SUOS, Energy Technology Support Unit, Harwell, Oxfordshire, 1982.

Givoni, B., 1976, 'Man, Climate and Architecture', Applied Science Publishers, London, 1987 (first edition 1969).

Hobday, R. A., Norton, B. & Probert, S. D., 1986, 'Retrofit passive solar air heating', Proc. 2nd UK-ISES Conference 'The Efficient Use of Energy in Buildings', Cranfield, Bedford, September 1986.

Hopkinson, R. G., Petherbridge, P. and Longmore, J., 1966, 'Daylighting', Heinemann, London, 1966.

Humphreys, N. A., 1978, 'Outdoor Temperatures and Comfort Indoors', BRE, Garston, Watford, UK, July 1978.

Kasabov, G., (Ed.) 1979, 'Buildings: The Key to Energy Conservation', RIBA, London 1979.

Loudon, A. G., & Langdon, F. J., 1970, 'Discomfort in Schools from Overheating in Summer', Journal of Institution of Heating and Ventilating Engineers, 37, p.265-274, 1970.

Norton, B. & Probert, S. D., 1984, 'Solar energy stimulated open-looped thermosyphonic air-heaters', Applied energy, 17, p.217-234, 1984.

Saint, A., 1987, 'Towards a Social Architecture, The role of School Buildings in Post-War England', Yale University Press New Haven and London, 1987, ISBN 0 300 038305.

Saxon, R., 1983, 'Atrium Buildings : Development and Design', Architectural Press, London, 1983.

Stonehouse, R. & Barbrook, R., 1984, 'Trio in Pitch', Architects Journal, 12 Dec.1984, p.31-52.

'Energy Conscious Design, A primer for architects', Batsford for the Commission of the European Communities, 1992, ISBN 0 7134 6919 6.

'Energy in Architecture: The European Passive Solar Handbook', 1992, Batsford, for the Commission of the European Communities, ISBN 0 7134 69188.

'Schools of Thought', Hampshire Architecture 1974 - 1991, Richard Weston, 1991 Hampshire County Council, ISBN 1 873595 10 7.

International Energy Agency: 'Solar Heating and Cooling -Task XI, Passive and Hybrid Solar Commercial Buildings', ISBN 0 442 21156 2, published by The Renewable Energy Promotion Group (REPG), Energy Technology Support Unit, Harwell, Oxfordshire.

Printed in the United Kingdom for HMSO
Dd 298308 C15 10/94 0559/1 59226